BLACK
Butterfly
Transform Your Pain into Your Purpose

Carla A. Vincent

ARCHWAY
PUBLISHING

Archway Publishing books may be ordered through booksellers or by contacting:

Archway Publishing
1663 Liberty Drive
Bloomington, IN 47403
www.archwaypublishing.com
844-669-3957

Because of the dynamic nature of the Internet, any web addresses or links contained in this book may have changed since publication and may no longer be valid. The views expressed in this work are solely those of the author and do not necessarily reflect the views of the publisher, and the publisher hereby disclaims any responsibility for them.

Any people depicted in stock imagery provided by Getty Images are models, and such images are being used for illustrative purposes only.
Certain stock imagery © Getty Images.

Scripture taken from the King James Version of the Bible.

Scripture quotations are from the ESV® Bible (The Holy Bible, English Standard Version®), copyright © 2001 by Crossway, a publishing ministry of Good News Publishers. Used by permission. All rights reserved.

Scripture quotations marked (NLT) are taken from the Holy Bible, New Living Translation, copyright © 1996, 2004, 2007 by Tyndale House Foundation. Used by permission of Tyndale House Publishers, Inc., Carol Stream, Illinois 60188. All rights reserved.

Scripture quotations marked (NIV) are taken from the Holy Bible, New International Version®, NIV®. Copyright © 1973, 1978, 1984, 2011 by Biblica, Inc.™ Used by permission of Zondervan. All rights reserved worldwide. www.zondervan.com The "NIV" and "New International Version" are trademarks registered in the United States Patent and Trademark Office by Biblica, Inc.™

ISBN: 978-1-6657-0453-3 (sc)
ISBN: 978-1-6657-0454-0 (hc)
ISBN: 978-1-6657-0455-7 (e)

Library of Congress Control Number: 2021905461

Print information available on the last page.

Archway Publishing rev. date: 07/06/2021

To my Lord and Savior, Jesus Christ.

To my sweet, loving, and caring life partner, life companion, heaven-sent angel, my "At Last," George Vincent.

To my sweet, loving babies: Omarion, Eli, Faith Angel, and Fluffy.

In loving memory of
Evelyn Sharp and Shavonne Sharp

*If you believe,
you will receive
whatever
you ask for
in prayer.*
Jesus

CONTENTS

FOREWORD

If you are looking to take your life to the next level, then this book is a must-read. Success is a journey that travels through a lot of trials and tribulations. Carla has been able to articulate what she's learned and pass it on by sharing her awe-inspiring story, going from pain to power.

This book will leave you feeling motivated and inspired while giving you some powerful strategies to implement in your life right away.

To whoever is reading this message, you have greatness within you; go out there and shine your light.

Carla, you are a blessing to this world. God bless you.

Eric Ho
International Speaker, Celebrity Entrepreneur, Author, Philanthropist

PREFACE

Shortly after my mentor gave me the mission to write a book, I began to brainstorm on possible topics. All of a sudden, the structure of the book and chapters began to pour out of me. It was like I could not stop writing. At that moment, I had not even considered a title. While outside playing with my children, I began to hum a tune and mumbled, "Black butterfly … set the sky on fire." I thought to myself, *Where did that come from and why was I singing it? I haven't heard that song in decades.*

Then it suddenly dawned on me: It was a divine message from God, because I had prayed to him to help me with the book. That was it! It was the title of my book. I researched the song because I couldn't remember all the lyrics. To my surprise, the song was released in 1984, when I was about five years old. I knew I had heard the song years after the release, but definitely not recent. Reviewing the lyrics confirmed it was the perfect title because the lyrics matched my life. Check out the excerpts from Deniece Williams (1984) "Black Butterfly." The complete lyrics of the song can be found on www.azlyrics.com/lyrics/deniecewilliams/blackbutterfly.html:

> You've survived, now your moment has arrived
> Now your dream has finally been born
>
> While you slept, the promise was unkept
> But your faith was as sure as the stars

Now you're free, and the world has come to see
Just how proud and beautiful you are

Write the timeless message clear across the sky
So that all of us can read it and remember when we need it.

In the Cocoon

The main verse truly resonated with me; it explained my life so beautifully. You see, I had been in a cocoon for many years, almost sleepwalking. I was so inactive mentally and spiritually after enduring many trials, tribulations, mistakes, heartache, and pain. I appeared to be okay on the outside, but inside, I was on sleep mode. A few months ago, my husband and I decided to start our own trucking company. I knew that I had the knowledge, education, and experience to write a business plan and get started on federal, state, and local requirements, but I had to remove the cobwebs, if you will, from my brain. I haven't used the knowledge in years, but I knew God could and would restore all of my memory and knowledge. So I prayed, and True Deliverance Holiness Church intercessory prayer group prayed as well. Let me tell you about the power of prayer: God began to flood my mind with knowledge each day.

I continued to pray and thought to myself, *There must be more to who I am.* I was more than glad to assist my husband pursue his dreams of owning and operating his own business. I knew it would fulfill him and financially benefit our family as well as demonstrate to our children the valuable lessons in entrepreneurship and pursuing your goals and dreams. While working hard on administrative duties, I could not help but to think, what about my own goals and dreams? Had I given up altogether? Because I suffered from severe depression, anxiety, and neck pain, did it mean my entire life was over? Was there more to me? Did God make all these provisions in my life just to sit, suffer, and be made useless? Were all the knowledge, education, experiences, and lessons that I learned throughout my lifetime in vain?

I knew there was more to me. As I thought to myself, I was in my late thirties and had no apparent talent or unusual skills. What was my purpose? Why was I here? So blessed beyond measure, yet so underutilized and so hidden. From time to time, I thought there was something more in me. It was so hidden within, I began to believe it had disappeared. Perhaps it was still not my season. So when was my season?

Some people are talented with skills that appear naturally at an early age. If someone were to ask me what I was good at, I would have to say, "Nothing." I could not sing or dance, but I did sew a bit as well as create arts and craft projects, and I was interested in acting; however, I had nothing that I was passionate enough to pursue. There was something I had not considered noteworthy, something that was much needed as well as in high demand, especially in a world with so much negativity, evil, hate, war, corruption, and chaos. What could be so hidden in plain sight? It was hidden treasure within me.

I started making social media videos about the law of attraction and received an overwhelmingly positive response from my followers, whom I called my divine connections. They appreciated my encouragement and the motivation I provided, which they responded to via comments, inbox messages, and phone calls. At that moment, I realized I was motivator. I was naturally a motivator, especially for family and friends.

So Blessed Beyond Measure

In the world we live in today, motivation, encouragement, and inspiration are needed to counteract and defeat all the negativity we regularly encounter. I understood that we must fight good with evil and claim the victory in advance. All this time, I was living a life here on earth, feeling like a zero, struggling just to be average but at times feeling so powerful.

There were times in my life I would have a feeling of discernment which led me to believe there was something different about me, something that I needed to explore, uncover, and share. My instincts were right. Some people even got the opportunity to witness this ability.

Metamorphosis: Cocoon to Butterfly

I decided I was breaking out of the cocoon I hid in for so long; I was going set the sky on fire. I analyzed the meaning of Deniece Williams's song, "Black Butterfly"; a black butterfly is believed to be a symbol of transformation, transition, renewal, or rebirth. The meaning was remarkably fitting for my life, because that's exactly what I had been going through the last several years: transformation (depressed to highly motivated); transition (working to retirement); renewal (feeling stagnant to being fulfill and vibrant).

It's a positive sign. The symbolism of a black butterfly and the song lyrics perfectly described my life's journey, especially since black butterflies are not as common as butterflies of other colors, meaning they are special, unique, and very rare. Below, I examine how the lyrics connect to my life:

> As the darkness gave way to dawn, you survived.
> Now your moment has arrived.
> Now your dream has finally been born.

You see, in 2005, I returned home from the war in Afghanistan, and for the next decade, I lived in denial of untreated depression, anxiety, and cervical pains. After I began to seek help of counseling and self-care, I could see the light, and brighter days were ahead. I decided to get more help to reveal my true self, which led me to write this book. It felt right, so natural, and meant to be.

> Black Butterfly, set the skies on fire, rise up even higher.

This verse is saying to be very successful, all will see your accomplishments.

While you slept, the promise was unkept
But your faith was as sure as the stars.
Now you're free, and the world has come to see
Just how proud and beautiful you are.

During that decade of suffering with the symptoms of depression, I dealt with isolation, fatigue, hopelessness, and hypersomnia. In addition to oversleeping, I was actually sleepwalking through life; through it all, I still trusted God for everything and remained faithful to him. I realized that I served a really big God, and he could make me completely whole again. I decided I needed to bust loose and become free from all these ailments and the darkness. I felt stuck and decided to invest in myself and get a mentor to help me out. Now I have friends all around the world, watching my videos. I have more confidence, and I am humbly proud of myself for stepping out on faith. Now, I can confidently declare that I am truly beautiful on the inside and outside and ready for the world see it.

Write your timeless message clear across the sky
So that all of can read it and remember when we need it
That a dream conceived in truth can never die.
Butterfly.

I am writing this book in hopes that people all around the world read it. They will be forever motivated, encouraged, and inspired by my words. My instincts told me there was more in me. In fact, there is so much more. I have a vision board that reflects big dreams, and they're unfolding right before my very eyes. The sky is the limit to what I can have.

ACKNOWLEDGMENTS

Archie Sharp Jr.
Bishop Nathaniel Wells Sr. and First Lady Mary A. Wells
Bishop Nolan Torbert and First Lady Diane Torbert
Bishop T. D. Jakes and First Lady Serita Jakes
Bob Procter
Cassie Singleton
Christy Whitman
Dara Anthony
Darnel Marble
Deniece Williams
Donald Lawrence
Dorinda Clark Cole
Eric Ho
Erick Robinson
Esther/Abraham-Hicks
Greater Harvest Baptist Church, Muskegon Heights, MI
Holy Trinity COGIC, Muskegon, MI
Jameka Marble
Dr. Judith Orloff
Karen Clark Sheard
Latasha Oliver
Marvin Sapp
Nadine Lenox
Natalie Ledwell, MindMovies

Nicole Houston (dba Nicc Hou)
Nina Simone
Oprah Winfrey
Peter Adams
Pharrell Williams
Rev. Ike Williams
Rhonda Byrne
Semper Fi Fund
Serwaah Coggins
Swendenborg
Tamela Mann
Teenee Frazier
Terri Savelle Foy
True Deliverance Holiness Church (TDHC), Auburn, AL
TDHC Intercessory Prayer Team
Wounded Warrior Program (WWP)

INTRODUCTION

In this book, I will my share world by revealing my outlook, my perception, my conditioning, and my experiences, as well as my realizations and revelations. I will discuss how I used the law of attraction, my spirituality, and my human body to manifest my heart's desires. For the purpose of this book, I will consider law of attraction as a part of science. It is one of the most popular universal laws. Some consider it to be a part of New Thought philosophy or metaphysics, others believe there is no scientific basis and has been dubbed a pseudoscience. The law of attraction states that "like attracts like" whether negative or positive.

Despite what some people believe, the law of attraction principles align with the spiritual beliefs of Christianity, as well as other religions. By effectively applying the Word of God, you can in fact drastically change your life for the better. The law of attraction teaches that what you think, you become. This principle is aligned with Proverbs 23:7 ("for as he thinks in his heart, so is he"). Furthermore, I will explain how I make use of my God-given human senses; there is power in expressing your thoughts and emotions, speaking life, using your imagination, writing your vision, and making your own choices.

Come on in and share my world, a world that once had many ups, downs, and turnarounds, but my world is just where it is supposed to be now, filled with love, compassion, understanding, and most importantly, wisdom. I came to realize that no matter which way my world was positioned, there was always a lesson to be learned. There was always favor and blessings from the Lord. He has always been watching over and guiding me.

For the longest time, I saw no real purpose in my life, but God knew all along. He saw the best in me when others only saw my flaws. Although many were healed and were blessed, he knew I would be one of the few to return to say, "Thank you, Lord." He knew my heart and soul would be overwhelmed with gratitude. He knew I would come back to tell the world everything he did for me. He knew I would share my testimony.

God knew I would encourage, inspire, and motivate the masses. He knew I was just the right person; he knew I loved and respected people regardless of ethnicity, race, religion, income, and region. He knew me better than I know myself.

I hope to impact all who have endured pain and would like to learn how to transform it into power. Everyone has experienced pain at some point in their life, but some are unable to see the light at the end of the tunnel. They become bound to the hurt and stay stuck in the past. I would like to show them that life can get better if they trust in God and do the work within themselves in order to move forward.

I still remember the song we sang in preschool about God having the whole wide world in his hand. It features children of different ethnicity uniting with each other. It was a beautiful concept. We are all God's people, whether you believe it or not. We are all connected. We are all spiritual beings having a human experience. Some consider the spirit as energy. That means we are all energy vibrating at different frequencies, according to Emanuel Swedenborg, a Swedish scientist, philosopher, religious teacher, and visionary. He claimed that since we are spiritual beings having a human experience, the soul is considered divine, where unconditional love, forgiveness, compassion, peace, happiness, and harmony reside. Our spirit is here to experience this life and its lessons. Swedenborg argued that we do not see ourselves as spiritual beings adopting a human experience but vice versa. We are all connected to a higher power, who is God.

We are essentially a spirit, who has a soul and lives in a body. Some consider the body as just a shell, while we in Christ consider our bodies as a sacred temple which must be a living sacrifice, holy, and pleasing to God. We all carry a spirit, whether pure or evil. Remember, in the beginning, God created the earth and Adam and Eve; we are all a result of his creation, meaning one way or another, we are connected. Our spirit is considered energy created by God; everything in this world is energy. Therefore, we are connected because everything is energy, only vibrating at different frequencies.

The law of attraction is not some bag of tricks; it is actually a lifestyle. It is not some hocus-pocus. It has absolutely helped me get a better understanding of the Word of God. Everyone on earth, no matter their ethnicity, race, or religion, is governed under the universal laws, whether they accept them or not. For instance, you would not jump off a cliff and expect to float in the air. No. You are aware of the law of gravity; what goes up must come down. Although we do not fully understand how it works, we believe in it and know how to abide by it. Well, the same should apply with the law of attraction; we need to know how to abide within the law in order to manifest our blessings.

The law of attraction allows people around the world to have a common ground to meet on. When I first became aware of the law of attraction and *The Secret,* Rhonda Byrne's book, I looked into the basics, to see if it aligned with my spiritual beliefs. I was immediately taken back and said to myself, "This is not a secret; this is the Word of God." Most notably, I recognized that they did not mention God, Jesus, or Holy Spirit; instead, they replaced God with the word "universe." It is my belief that God created the universe and all that exists, so I worship and pray to the Creator, not what he created. While I do not accept praying to the universe, the fact remains, I could locate scriptures for all the law of attraction's principles.

Does that mean I throw out the entire concept because it refers to the universe? No way. What remained constant was that these were effective methods and strategies to incorporate the Word of God in my everyday life, not just on Sundays. What was obvious to me was that a lot of Christians didn't know how to implement the Word of God in action. It has been my experience that Christians were some of the sickest and brokest people, yet they spend hours a week at church. I have witnessed  some miraculous events but nowhere near what the scriptures promised. While some churches are loud and upbeat, filled with high emotions, and the preacher speaks amazing messages, most people still went home broke, sick, and depressed. For many, the message went in one ear and out the other. I knew there had to be something more, especially since the scripture said so. I came to understand that we are very powerful beings; however, many people walk around every day feeling powerless, underutilizing their true power, and ignoring the authority that lies within themselves.

I wrote this book to help people realize their power within; I have explained each of the key components of the law of attraction and my experience applying them. I also reveal my musical inspirations that help with application of the law. Each chapter includes a section on spirituality, where I provide the most inspirational Bible verses as well as relevant quotes from other religions. As I reveal my world through the upcoming chapters, you will see how music enhanced the manifestation process for me.

According to my research and experience, music can raise your vibration to the highest frequency. If you would like to increase your energy level, achieve the state of joy, or open your heart and soul, you can use music to raise your vibration through uplifting and empowering lyrics as well upbeat tones. Have you ever listened to a song that takes

This is not a secret, "this is the Word of God"

you back to a specific memory, time, place, or person? Music has the power to make us feel all kinds of emotions.

For instance, if you listen to a song that make you feel sad, your vibrations and thoughts will align with those negative feelings. Or if you listen to motivating music, your vibrations and thoughts will align with positive feelings, making it easier to manifest your heart's desires. It is important to choose music and sounds that resonate good feelings.

You will learn how I intentionally use my God-given human body functions and processes to manifest my desire by ensuring I monitor what I see (eyes), feel (heart), think (brain), imagine (mind), speak (mouth), write (hands), and so much more. By the use of vision boards, affirmations, visualizations, inspired actions, gratitude, love, and forgiveness for biblical application in my daily life, I was able to manifest my blessings. I am sure if you actively apply similar approaches, you too will be able to manifest before you know it. As I previously stated, the law of attraction, like the Word of God, is a lifestyle. Whether you realize it or not, the law of attraction is always at work. Let's get deliberate manifesting our blessings. At the end of each chapter is an exercise to help you start applying the law of attraction today.

1

See It Before You See It

Any manifestation starts with seeing something; if you have an idea, you have to imagine, then believe, then visualize in your mind before you see it with your physical eyes. You have to live in that moment of what you have been desiring. The Word of God even tells us to declare the end from the beginning (Isaiah 46:10); it says that God plans to give us an expected end (Jeremiah 29:11). One of God's prophets even encourages us to write the vision and make it plain, and that it will surely come (Habakkuk 2:1–3).

Does that mean these ancient scriptures no long apply today? No, of course not. They still apply today because the Word of God is alive and active. We just have to apply it properly, do it consistently, and most importantly believe the Word the God. That's where the law of attraction techniques and methods help with biblical application. One method is scripting; in this powerful tool, you write down your future as if it had already happened, the expected end. It's like stepping into a movie written by you. Be sure to be specific and include every little detail. Have the audacity to dream big.

- ❑ Be clear about what you want.
- ❑ Why do you want it?
- ❑ How does it feel to have it?
- ❑ Make it believable.
- ❑ Be grateful now.

Scripting Your Future

Scripting is a perfect example of declaring the end from the beginning. It is a great way to use your imagination and visualization techniques; it's also very fun to do. Just like the title of this chapter, you see it, before you see it. It's like writing your own movie that you star in. It's an opportunity to have the audacity to think and dream big. Remember, we serve a big God who is able to make the impossible possible. We just have to believe, know, and stand on his Word. In the section below, you will see how I boldly and specifically use my imagination to script my desired end vision. It was quite a fun exercise, to say the least.

Living at the End

As Antoinette Victorious stood backstage, awaiting her turn to speak to the largest audience she's ever been in front of, the last couple of years of her life flashed before her eyes. Her eyes began to fill with tears; she tried her best to hold them back so she wouldn't mess up her professional makeup. She was overwhelmed with gratitude for all that God had done for her. As she stood there, it felt like she was in a dream, yet she felt so alive like never before. She thought to herself, *It actually worked.* Then she repeated under her breath, "It actually worked." No one would ever believe her.

How could she ever explain this magnificent transformation? Her own mind was blown, and those around her were also shocked. This sudden transformation in her life was astonishing, to say the least. It was her ideal of a total successful life. It's a good thing she had four witnesses who had always been in her life: George, her husband, their two sons, Omarion and George Jr., and Faith Angel, their daughter.

The average person would say her routine was crazy, weird, or faith-driven, or she was just blessed beyond measure.

No matter what they said, they could not deny the fact that she suddenly became a multimillionaire, a best-selling author, an international empowerment speaker, coach, and entrepreneur. Her husband and children had witnessed many times before how things had manifested in her life, but definitely not on this level. They knew she was special. They knew she was a powerhouse. They knew she was straight fire. They knew that her meditation time was consistent. Her praise and worship at home and church were the same. She never revealed to them how she meditated or what she actually did in her prayer closet. She had a routine of praying, reading the Bible and other prayer books, meditating, journaling, doing law of attraction exercises, and writing gratitude lists. She also had implemented visualization and imagination processes. Would her family even believe that everything they were experiencing was the result of her own imagination?

Her family did, in fact, witness when the prize patrol delivered a giant check after she won a sweepstakes. Her family was in shock and speechless; they heard her speak of winning, acting out the prize-winning day, praying, and thanking God for it in advance, and they saw her poster of her receiving the winnings.

She was indeed the largest prize winner that company ever had; she received a total of seven monetary prizes. Upfront she received a check for $10 million and expected to receive three hundred thousand dollars monthly for her lifetime, then after that, for the lifetime of a beneficiary designated by her. You see, she knew she would win in perfect timing. She even had a bank account set up and hired an accountant and lawyer to ensure she and her family were legally and financially protected. Again, did her family really know? It was not coincidence or luck. She actually had affirmations of that exact statement. She visualized the day down to the details in her mind. Her older son, Omarion, even asked if she was psychic. She explained that she had embraced the power of the mind, the power of praise and worship, and the power of prayer, all of which were the power of God, and she became in total alignment with her desires.

As she waited to speak, the flashes of memories continued. She thought of how she had imagined her hairstyle, her makeup, her custom-made outfit, as well as the red heels she wore. She had the exact images screenshot in her phone. You see, she had actually seen herself wearing it, in her mind. She felt herself touching the fabric. She felt it clinging to her body. She even felt the soft, luxurious weave in her hair. She noticed the people who admired her as she walked past. The only difference was it was reality. The line between imagination and reality was blurred.

She had even imagined the high vibrations in the arena, filled with thousands of her divine connections; it gave her even more power to motivate them. It was pure energy surging throughout the place, and she felt it all. She even imagined how they would receive her message and go on to manifest great things for themselves. Her faith, which is believing in the things that were not seen, was now reality. She actually pinched herself at that moment just to be sure.

She felt the pinch; it was all real. She was now living in her true divine purpose. Some would even call what she did a ministry. She was spreading the good news to people all across the world. She was telling them about the goodness and power of God. She was encouraging, inspiring, and motivating God's people to rise up, take their position, and become aware of their power within. It felt so mystical to her to be living on purpose, in her purpose.

One of the many advantages of being a multimillionaire was that she could make their dream home their reality, with all the details. The new home they recently built was an exact match of the images she had imagined. Everything down to the mansion's external brick and beautifully manicured lawn. The foyer had cream and gold accented moldings, and the home had a spacious open floor plan; cream marble tile was throughout the home. The plush carpet in each bedroom felt like you were walking on clouds. Their master suite was fit for a royal king and queen, which they were.

Everything was so elegant and luxurious. Their multicar garage contained his-and-her Escalade Cadillacs as well as an Aston Martin sport car and Bentley, the same ones she had imagined. Now she and her family traveled around the world for weeks at a time, exploring all that God created. She and her family experienced many adventures and cultures around the world together. She was also paid a lucrative income for speaking engagements. This is what she had posted on her vision board.

As she waited her turn to speak, she became mesmerized by her own life and how God had orchestrated everything she had written down and visualized. At that same moment, she received multiple phone notifications about all the deposits in their multiple business ventures. She quickly checked her account balance and counted eight figures. Her eyes bulged in shock. The shock came because it was significant growth in their bank account due to the book sales and network marketing sales. Even after winning the sweepstakes and becoming a multimillionaire, she intended to continue with their business plans.

They no longer had any debt, so they were living the paid-in-full lifestyle that she had many times affirmed. They were earning the income she had spoken about. Due to her sudden fame and manifested wealth, their family businesses were household names around the world; people were drawn to her and her life story, and they wanted to be a part of her team. They wanted to be connected to her in some way. Her divine connections knew everything associated with her was blessed, even those who were part of their marketing networks.

She was one of the most influential people in the world. Being the intelligent woman that she was, she capitalized on it. She had no shame in her retention of wealth and riches. For she did not take a vow of poverty; in addition, she had experienced poverty during her younger years.

They controlled their money; their money did not control them. She believed God when he said, "For it is he that giveth thee power to get wealth" (Deuteronomy 8:18). You see, she knew that God never lied. She had been thoroughly taught by one of her spiritual leaders, Bishop Wells, that it is impossible for God to lie. Armed with that strong consolation, she knew she could stand firm on his Word and that he would deliver on his promises as long as she abided in his Word and his will.

They were also philanthropists. They applied the law of reaping and sowing into their life. For the Word of God and the law of attraction stressed giving, and they did so generously; because of that, she and her family lived every day in the overflow of blessings. They gave a million dollars to the following charities because they affected her either directly or indirectly:

- American Cancer Society
- American Diabetes Association
- Domestic Violence Association
- Sickle Cell Disease Association

Few people knew about the organizations they gave to because they donated in secret. She was most hesitant about giving in public but due to their businesses and brand management, they needed to give publicly as well. Some people criticized them about their giving, saying they should give more; however, they had no direct knowledge of her donation, nor would she appease them by giving details. Instead, the critics would watch from the front row as more blessings poured in.

Most philanthropists just threw money at people in impoverished locations. She had a project to educate people throughout the world on the universal laws (as well as the Word of God), teaching them how to activate their mind power as well as implement the laws into their daily lives. Her plan was to teach them how to help themselves and create a sustainable lifestyle. She also bought a building to establish a homeless shelter for veterans and domestic violence victims (areas of life she was familiar with).

Antoinette Victorious and her family always stayed in suites at the most luxurious five-star hotels. They were chauffeured around to the best places each country had to offer. Since she needed her family by her side, they got the best nanny and best tutor for the children's education. This was most people's dream life, but this was their reality. They were treated like royalty. In fact, she was royalty; her father was God, and she was his daughter. She realize this as a young girl when the Lord made so many provisions for her while her biological father was in prison. She knew that he was King of Kings and Lord of Lords and the Alpha and the Omega. He had poured out a blessing that she did not have room enough to receive. She had to share her wisdom and knowledge with the world.

She also shared her financial blessings with her extended family. They were all excited about their upcoming trip; she arranged to travel to two major cities. She had gotten them the best charter bus along with best hotels to stay in. A major family trip that they had only dreamed about was going to be their reality.

She hired home health care for her paternal grandmother. She also bought a home for her aunt, who helped raised her and was like a mother to her. This aunt helped her through many difficult times by displaying love and giving her the hugs she desperately needed. This aunt had always looked out for her, wherever she was in the world. She also bought a mini-mansion for her aunt, cousins, and family to stay in as they wished.

She bought her auntie a Cadillac Escalade in gratitude for everything that she had done for their family. For her maternal grandmother, she purchased a brand-new home as well as a family van. Antoinette was now living her best life from that point to forever more. She had total success in all aspects of her life. It was not just the money. She felt great about living her purpose, being fulfilled, and helping others as well as having a healthy, happy family and living her life to the fullest. The Word of God was definitely manifested in her life; her latter days were greater than her former (Job 8:7).

A year prior, she was stuck and felt bored by her dull routine. Although she loved taking care of her family, she knew she had more to give. She knew she had more to offer her family as well as to the world. She knew that God had not brought her that far to leave her with all the knowledge, wisdom, and experience that she gained throughout the years. She knew she was special. She knew she was different from others. She also knew that she needed help to get to the next level of her life.

She decided to invest in herself. She realized that she was more than enough, even though at times she felt less than. She collaborated with her mentor, who was a successful entrepreneur, speaker, coach, philanthropist, and author. This multimillionaire saw greatness in her immediately and even said that she was a powerhouse. He activated her by encouraging her to go beyond her comfort zone. He pushed her out of the nest. She did not fall to the ground and die; she actually spread her wings and began to fly like an eagle. It was her season to soar high.

For so long, everyone saw only her flaws. But just like Marvin Sapp's song said, "He [God] saw the best in her." While everyone else wrote her off as nothing, God had plans to magnify her in due season; he tremendously magnified her territory, just like Jabez in 1 Chronicles 4:9. While everyone else saw her for who she used to be, God saw her for who she would be. She needed to see the best within herself. Who was she to go against what God said? Yes, she made many mistakes in her past. Now it was about getting it right, turning those mistakes into lessons, helping others, and staying on the righteous path. She needed to speak, believe, think, and be the best that God knew she was. Since the Lord said she was, she was, so until these things began to manifest, she began to speak it into the atmosphere, saying:

"I am blessed in the city. I am blessed in the country. My products and services are blessed. My business expansion is blessed. My investments are blessed. My children are blessed. My food is blessed. My land is blessed. My work is blessed. My stores are blessed. I lend to many nations. I am blessed when I come in. I am blessed when I go out. I am the head and not the tail. I am above and not beneath."

Yes, she and her family were living Deuteronomy 28 life to the fullest.

Who knew that she was a real superhero, with superpowers and enough energy to share with the world? She was needed in a world filled with so much chaos and negative spirits. After being down for so long, it was now her time to rise up and shine. She was powerful. Her mind had great power. All those times when she felt so powerless and helpless, everything she needed was inside of her. She knew that the same power inside her was inside of all her divine connections, but she needed to activate them the way she had been activated. She had to pay it forward by passing on this knowledge and insight. Her divine connections needed to know they were also powerful. They needed to realize that power and use it. They too could utilize the power of God, along with the laws of the universe, to manifest their dreams into reality, but they must become conscious of the power within them.

So many thoughts and flashes of memories went through her mind that she almost missed her cue to go on stage. The crowd went crazy as she walked out like the superstar of motivation she was, a divine diva. She felt the crowd's powerful energy; however, she was still so nervous. Her palms were sweaty, and her heart raced. When she saw her life partner and children in the front row, looking so proud, smiling from ear to ear, a sense of calm immediately came over her. It was like she was a totally different person. It was like déjà vu, the feeling of having experienced that moment already. It was possible because she had the exact replica of everything in her mind. Who was this woman who had been catapulted to such great heights so suddenly? Well, she is me, and I am her.

Join me as God orchestrates my desires, and they unfold in perfect timing. Watch me as I continue to transform; I will fly high and set the sky on fire. I was once unknown, but now I am unforgettable.

Spirituality

Declaring the end from the beginning, and from ancient times the things that are not yet done, saying, My counsel shall stand, and I will do all my pleasure. (Isaiah 46:10)

For I know the thoughts that I think toward you, saith the LORD, thoughts of peace, and not of evil, to give you an expected end. (Jeremiah 29:11)

And the LORD answered me, and said, write the vision, and make it plain upon tables, that he may run that readeth it. For the vision is yet for an appointed time, but at the end it shall speak, and not lie: though it tarry, wait for it; because it will surely come, it will not tarry. (Habakkuk 2:2–3)

Exercise

Chosen one or two of these life areas to focus on:

- ❑ spiritual
- ❑ physical
- ❑ financial
- ❑ career
- ❑ relationship

Consider what you like the end goal to be for your chosen life areas. Using the scripting technique, write a story about your life based on how you want it to be. (Use extra paper as needed.)

_____

_____

_____

_____

_____

_____

_____

_____

_____

_____

2

I Speak Life into Existence

" In the beginning was the Word, and the Word was God" (John 1:1 King James Version). This well-known Bible verse teaches us that everything begins with the spoken word. God gave us that same power and authority. We need to walk in that power and authority so we can call forth spiritual things into the natural realm. The Word of God also tells us that God uses words to "call those things which are not as though they were." So we must do the same; rather than telling it like is it, speak by faith as it will be.

While our thoughts also impact what we manifest in our lives, the real power lies in our words. Our innermost thoughts, when spoken in a  bold affirmation, can manifest into a reality. So it is important that we choose our words wisely by thinking consciously about what we speak. We can affirm who we are or who we desire to be by using two small words yet incredibly powerful words: "I am." It is also important to speak with positive emotions to give the affirmation more power to manifest quicker.

If you fail to realize your power, your statements will attract into your life the very circumstances you want to avoid (lack or scarcity or illness). So instead of saying, "I am broke," make a statement like, "I am financially secure." The Bible even stated that we are snared by the words of our mouth, meaning we trap ourselves by what we say. Our words eventually keep us from God's promises of things to come. The moment we speak something out of our mouth or believe it in our heart (good or bad), we've given life to it.

Self-Talk

So do you talk to yourself? Self-talk is the practice of talking to yourself, either out loud or silently. Some people are unaware that they do it. I know that I do it often, both aloud and internally. One day, I spoke to someone about the importance of monitoring what we say amongst ourselves. They said they didn't talk to themselves but always talked to God. First, since

God is in us, I definitely agreed with that statement, because whether we think we're talking to ourselves or to God, he still hears it.

Well, for the rest of us who are not so deep and spiritual, the question is, how do you talk to yourself? What are you saying about your circumstances, situation, events, or people? How you talk to yourself is important because you are the one listening. I consider this a form of speaking; we must ensure our self-talk is positive, because God and the universe is listening, and what we say will manifest. Remember, we are powerful beings.

My Experience with Speaking Life

Part of being aware of what you're saying is understanding the concept of speaking life. I often say, "I claim it, I believe it, I see it, and I receive it, in Jesus's name, Amen," declaring also it is done. The meaning of these words is explained below:

- I claim it: It is mine already.
- I believe it: I accept it as true.
- I see it: I see it (in the spiritual realm) before I actually see it in the natural realm (stage of my mind).
- I receive it: I welcome it into my life.

There's a scripture I memorized: "Death and life are in the power of the tongue: and they that love it shall eat the fruit thereof" (Proverbs 18:21 KJV). However, when it came to applying the verse in everyday life, it was not always clear. But after learning from the law of attraction that our spoken words have power and vibrate on a spiritually level as well as a physical level, it all started to make sense. Because according to the law of attraction, when we think, believe, feel, and speak something (positive or negative), we draw in more of that vibration. So by knowing that, I consciously monitor my senses to ensure I am in high-frequency emotions such as happy, peace, love, and gratitude to manifest my desires. I am currently working to stay aligned with my next goals. While affirmations have worked in the past, I feel like I am ready to implement other manifesting tools such as visualization and meditation.

My Musical Inspiration

The gospel artist Donald Lawrence's 2006 song "I Speak Life" helped get me through a rough patch in my life. His song reminded me that I had the power to speak life over myself, and so I did (and I still do today). I encourage you to do the same. Some excerpts of the lyrics are below (the complete lyrics can be found on www.azlyrics.com/lyrics/donaldlawrence/ispeaklife.html):

> We're livin' in a time, where everybody is strugglin' for their lives. They're stressed, they're depressed …
>
> I speak life, you're gonna live, Oh, my brother, my sister.
> I speak life, you are the head and not the tail, you will prevail.
> I speak life, don't give up the fight for your life, you shall live and not die.

Spirituality

Here are a few religious verses that display how speaking positive words is important in most cultures and religions:

> Death and life are in the power of the tongue: and they that love it shall eat the fruit thereof. (Proverbs 18:21 KJV)
>
> Choose the best words to speak and say them in the best possible way. (Quran 2:83, 17:53)
>
> Speak only endearing speech that welcomes. Speech, when it brings no evil to others, is a pleasant thing. (Buddha)

Exercise

Let me help you get started today by transforming your life with your words. Using the example below, develop positive statements in each of your major life areas.

Spiritual: _____

_____

_____

Physical: _____

_____

_____

Financial: _____

_____

_____

Career: _____

_____

_____

Relationship: _____

_____

_____

Negative Statement	Positive Statement
I am broke.	I am in the process of gaining
I am sick and tired.	financial stability.
I am not enough.	I am healthy and energetic now.
	I am more than enough now.

3

The Importance of Gratitude

G ratitude can truly transform your life. It is a powerful exercise of the law of attraction; however, people often forget to use it. A *Forbes* study revealed gratitude has several benefits (Morin, 2014):

- It opens the door to more relationships.
- It improves physical health.
- It improves psychological health.
- It enhances empathy and reduces aggression.
- It help you to sleep better.
- It improves your self-esteem.
- It increases mental strength.

With all these benefits, one would think expressions of gratitude would be used frequently. Especially since etiquette is one of the first things we learn as small children. Gratitude is proper etiquette. It is important to recognize others. It demonstrates that we acknowledge our relationship with that person. It is a social nicety. So why do people disregard this basic but important lesson? Some people may think they're too busy with their daily lives. Perhaps they don't realize that failing to say thank you is a clear sign of ingratitude. It's not only considered rude, it can impact their relationships and discourage further blessings or kind acts in the future.

In the law of attraction, gratitude is an energy that returns to you magnified, which basically means:

> To attract more of what you want in life is to
> be grateful for what you already have.

That means to be present in the moment, to appreciate and be content right now with what you have, no matter how little or big. You should express your gratitude to family, friends, strangers, or anyone else who warrants it; it is especially important to express gratitude to the creator of everything, God.

As previously mentioned, the expression of gratitude is very powerful and is a high-energy emotion on the emotional vibrational frequency chart (see exhibit 8.1). I recently became aware of this chart and found it very intriguing; I intend to incorporate in my practice and strategies when manifesting with the law of attraction. As some might know, we are all vibrational beings, always sending out signals, intentional or unintentionally. Remember, like attracts like; therefore, what vibrations we send out, we attract back into our lives. Although we all have a range of emotions, the goal is to reach the next emotion up the chart and to become more consistent at that level and continue to move higher.

My Experience in Gratitude

I was raised to be polite and always display gratitude by saying thank you. I also raised my kids to do the same. If my oldest son didn't thank me after I gave him something, I would ask for it back. I gave him a gift one day, and he didn't say thanks, and he even displayed a bad attitude. I wanted to take it back, because he was not appreciative or grateful. At that moment, I didn't want to give him any more gifts. However, if he expressed sincere gratitude, I would want to do more for him.

Well, the same matter applies with God, our Father, who created the universe. So whether we believe in God or his creation, the universe, the importance of expressing gratitude is still the same. If we stop worrying about our problems and begin to count our blessings and be grateful for everything, everyone, even every situation because we know this one thing that the testing of our faith come to make you strong and that all things work together for your good. When you go through the fire, you will come out as pure gold.

One year, during the Christmas holidays, I decided to increase my giving spirit and provide gifts to a group of people. While I didn't personally deliver the gifts, the twenty-five recipients were aware that I had sent them. Only one, yes, one person, contacted me to express gratitude for my gift. So who do you think was on the Christmas list the following year? That's right, the one who came back to express appreciation. I was so impressed with their acknowledgment but shocked at the lack of gratitude by the others. Needless to say, a simple thank you to anyone can go a long way and will increase your blessings.

One of the highest forms of gratitude is to praise God. I am a praiser. Praise is what I do. I am loud, energetic, powerful, and determined to get my praise and prayers through to God. Praising the Lord is definitely for me. I always say to myself, "From my lips to God's ear." As we now know, there is power in gratitude. Praise is a form of gratitude. Unfortunately, this is a struggle in many churches today. I believe that people are either scared or ashamed to praise the Lord in their house of worship, which is one of the main reasons for attending. I believe this because that was once me. I was not familiar with praising. It was out of my comfort zone, until I learned how important it is. It was not about my comfort or anyone else's; it was about giving God the glory that he so deserves.

If people only knew that there is power in their praise. While in praise, you are high in the Spirit; your vibrations are very high. You are fully exalting the Lord, expressing your best appreciation, at which chains are broken and healing takes place; deliverance happens. You get your blessings and breakthrough. Instead of getting all that praise has to offer, people remain in their comfort zone; it holds them back. They allow the fear of what others might say to hold them back. They simply do not trust the process.

Many times, I see a few praisers in church who watch rather than participate in the purpose of being there. The reason being to praise and worship, to receive God's Word, and to fellowship amongst other saints. Praise and gratitude are definitely not just for Sundays or for a select few individuals. They are for everyone, every day. Clearly, it is important because the word *praise* is mentioned in the Bible 259 times. Wow. So we should start praising and worshiping God more passionately. Let our praise be for real. If we truly contemplated on the goodness of God and all he has done for us, we all should burst through the doors to glorify him.

My Musical Inspiration

Marvin Sapp's "Praise Him in Advance" (2007) says to thank God now for what you are expecting. Why wait, if you believe? If you truly believe, you would get excited now. You would thank God now. Did you know that gratitude speeds up the manifestation? Remember, gratitude is one the highest vibrational emotions, meaning it is very powerful. I know a lot people who say, "I will be happy when …" Well, newsflash: You must be happy and grateful now. While you're waiting on him, he's waiting on you to believe him, trust him, give him glory, acknowledge his abilities and power, and know that he alone is God.

Prove this to him by sincerely saying thank you now. Watch how circumstances and situations begin to work in your favor. Below are some excerpts of "Praise Him in Advance" lyrics; for the complete lyrics, check out www.azlyrics.com/lyrics/marvinsapp/praisehiminadvance.html:

I've had my share of ups and downs, times
when there was no one around,
God came and spoke these words to me, praise will confuse the enemy.

So I started singing, I started clapping, I started
dancing, people were laughing,
they knew my problems, they knew my pain,
but I knew God would take them away.

That's why I praise him with my hands, that's
why I praise him with a dance,
He's given me a second chance, come on let's praise him in advance.

That's why I praise him with a song, when things
are right and when they're wrong,
He's given me a second chance, come on let's praise Him in advance.

Why wait, if you believe God is able to provide for your needs as well as desires, according to his will? You have to make a shift in your mind from asking to expecting the blessings of the Lord. It is a very powerful act; however, many people actually doubt and fear. I used to be like that, until my mentality shifted and I recalled that the spirit of fear and doubt is not from the Lord. God says through his Word that you must have faith and believe; he even said you only need faith as small as a mustard seed. Did you know that a mustard seed is the smallest of all seeds on earth, yet when planted, it grows and becomes the largest of all garden plants? God only requires a little faith from you that he can multiply into huge blessings.

The Bible offers a great illustration of how the Israelites overcame an obstacle to their new life. It was an actual wall, the walls of Jericho. The Israelites received instructions from their leader. They followed the instruction as ordered by God (you can review the story on your own in Joshua 1–6). The point I'd like to discuss is that they made a great shout, and the wall fell down flat. They had faith in the process. They trusted God. It is my belief that shouting and blowing the trumpet was an act of praising God for what they knew he would do: keep his promise. The walls came down, and they walked into their blessing.

In that same matter, we must open our mouth and shout praises to the King of Kings and Lord of Lords; he is able to deliver us, save us, heal us, and provide all that we need. I know for myself, praising and celebrating in advance works. Marvin Sapp's "Praise Him in Advance" helped me with that. That song was very encouraging and inspiring. I will be forever grateful to him for sharing his God-given gifts.

Spirituality

The word *thanks* or *thanksgiving* is mentioned more than a hundred times in the Bible. One of them is repeated below, along with a verse from the Quran and a quote from Buddha, showing that expressing gratitude crosses all cultures and religions.

> Give thanks to the Lord, for he is good; his love
> endures forever. (1 Chronicles 16:34 NIV)

If you are grateful, I shall certainly increase you. (Quran 14:7)

A noble person is mindful and thankful for the
favors he receives from others. (Buddha)

Learning for Others

As I accumulated knowledge about the law of attraction, I came across Terri Foy Savelle; she made the connection between the Word of God and the law of attraction, and she also noticed how some celebrities drastically transformed their lives by applying these principles. She spoke of her experience and described how she manifested items on her vision board. I had previously made a vision board, and Terri inspired me to update my vision and make my board bigger, better, and more specific. Throughout her YouTube series, she gives great advice as well as biblical applications.

In one video, she speaks about the importance of expressing gratitude and describes how her experience and upbringing led her to write handwritten thank-you notes whenever someone sends her a gift. After seed planting into her ministry, I received a sweet hand-written note for my gift. It was very touching and made me want to give continuously. I know that ministry will continue to grow because she has all the right ingredients and is actively applying God's Word while encouraging others to so do.

Exercise

Let's begin expressing gratitude today.

List three items in each of the major areas of life that you are presently grateful for or thanking God in advance for.

Spiritual: _____
_____
_____
_____

Physical: _____
_____
_____
_____

Financial: _____
_____
_____
_____

Career: _____
_____
_____
_____

Relationship: _____
_____
_____

4

Get Crystal Clear

H ave you ever been indecisive about what you wanted? Whether it was finances, a career, relationships, or love, I know I have been there, done that. Well, according to the law of attraction, you must get very clear on the specifics and details (the features, the amount, the when and where), because if you don't know exactly what you want, you can't take steps to make it happen. Most people do not know what they really want. According to Rhonda Byrne's *The Secret* (2006), when you see other people or things, it's like a catalog for you to pick and choose your own details. There are some people who look at what others have manifested with admiration, while others are mad and jealous.

One of my favorite scriptures says, "You receive not, because you ask not." So wait: You are looking at other people's blessings with hidden negative emotions, but you don't even know what you want in the first place, then on top of that, you never even asked God for anything. Stop right here, and allow me to help you get crystal clear on your desires. You must get clarify your desires to effectively manifest them and then proceed to ask God for them.

For example, rather than saying, "I want a big house," say, "I want a four-thousand-square-foot home with six bedrooms and four baths."

So once you are crystal clear, then you can ask God for what you want to manifest. He will begin to orchestrate your desires, if they are aligned with his will, in perfect time. If you don't ask, he may still help you out, but perhaps not as you intended. People often say, "Be careful what you ask for because you just might get it."

In my opinion, if you're not clear about your desires, it's like placing an order at a drive-through restaurant; after receiving your items, you say, "Thank you," and drive off, only to realize it's not what you wanted to order. You wanted something else entirely. You cannot go back; the line is full, and you'd have to drive around and wait. By then, you are frustrated with your order, which only brings more feelings of frustration. You got what you ask for, but you placed an unclear order. No returns, no refunds.

The Bible tells us, "Ask, and it will be given to you; seek, and you will find; knock, and the door will be opened to you," and it goes on to say that if you lack something, it's because you did not ask God for it. After incorporating the law of attraction methods into my spiritual walk, I learned to be specific with my requests. For example, I specifically asked God to bless me with someone who was just right for me. I received my request and now have a great life partner; I'm still in awe with him. I learned how to actively apply biblical principles in my daily life. It has been quite effective in manifesting my desires after getting clear on my desires and has helped me formulate affirmations. Later, I will discuss how writing affirmations has helped transform my life.

My Experience

My first encounter with the law of attraction was a free coaching session from Quantum Success Coaching with Christy Whitman. Yes, free. I wanted to see what it was all about. I was going through a very difficult transition in my life and needed help to get on track. For this coaching session, I focused on my time and energy; little did I know that in the next two years, my desires concerning my finances and health care

> To manifest what you want in life, you must first be clear about what that is.

I applied the same strategy for my love life, a new home, and more children. Long story short: I met and married the best guy for me, bought a brand-new home, and gave birth to another angel. Wow. Amazing, right? All of this manifested from that free session, my own inquiry into the law of attraction, biblical application, faith, and prayer.

Now that I was in a better financial position, what if I actually purchased the coaching services? The free guidance was great; I listened, took notes, and followed detailed instructions. What would come out of the paid services? In this book, I will explain how I leveled up by investing in myself.

You see, most people talk about what they do not want more than what they want. I learned this in my first session. Then, I was told to think of one area of my life that I wanted to work on. At the time, it was my finances. After positive circumstances started to manifest in my finances, I applied the same process to other areas of my life. You should do same. Below, I will give an example of the contrast (do not want) and clarity (do want).

Spirituality

The Bible explains about making your request to God:

> Be careful for nothing; but in everything by prayer and supplication with thanksgiving let your requests be made known unto God. (Philippians 4:6 KJV)

> Ye have not, because ye ask not. (James 4:2 KJV)

> Ask, and it shall be given you; seek, and ye shall find; knock, and it shall be opened unto you. (Matthew 7:7 KJV)

> Delight yourself in the LORD, and He will give you the desires of your heart. (Psalm 37:4 ESV)

Exercise

Start with one major life category (Spiritual, Physical, Financial, Career, Relationships), state what you don't want in the Contrast category. In the Clarity category, state what you would like, instead.

Contrast	Clarity
Example: No long work hours	Work eight hours a day
Example: Earn a lot of money	Earn $250,000 a year

Now that you've gotten clear on your desires, see the chart in the next chapter to write affirmations that resonate with you.

5

The Power of the Pen

After getting clear on your desires, now you should have the start of the affirmations. According to Habakkuk, the Lord said, "Write the vision, and make it plain upon tables, that he may run that readeth it," meaning clearly write down on paper whatever you want to be revealed, so clear and legible that whoever reads it may run to tell all the good news of what has manifested. Well, let me make a boast in the Lord and tell you that I have affirmations as well as vision boards that would make you run. And guess what? There are more amazing blessings to come for me and my family and you, too, if you decide to get clear, focus, and consistently manifest your desires.

Now that you are sure of your mission, you should start creating short and powerful affirmations by using words that convey power, energy, and enthusiasm.

Examples

- I love knowing that …
- I get excited when …
- I love the thought …
- I love how it feels …
- I love knowing …
- I love the idea …

For example, "I love knowing that I have total success in my life now."

The Next Step after Getting Clarity

"I love knowing that I only work eight hours per day."

Affirmations are positive statements that can help us to challenge and overcome self-sabotaging and negative thoughts. As you repeat them, you start to believe in them, and then you can start to make positive changes. When writing affirmations, it is important to design statements that work for you. They should feel good and be believable to you. You should read your affirmations daily with feelings. When you write an affirmation, you express your thoughts and emotions, releasing high vibrations. As you repeat writing and saying the affirmations, they enter your subconscious. Remember, if you want to add power to your affirmations in a big way, you need to include one simple ingredient: emotion.

My Experience in Writing

I know that this chapter is entitled "The Power of the Pen," but let me tell you how lipstick worked, too. Yes, lipstick on the mirror. In addition to speaking my affirmations, I would write my top two keywords from those affirmations on the mirror; that way, every time I looked in the mirror, I would see them and say them. With the mirror method, I manifested a promotion, a home, and another baby boy. I'm currently using this method for my current desires. It may seem drastic or weird to some, but I was asking for drastic blessings and expecting them. Below, I will name a few blessings that I was able to manifest using the Word of God and the law of attraction, but there is so much more.

Manifestation: Promote Me

Before I was aware of the law of attraction, I was still practicing it because of reading the Bible. My faith was strong, and I was being actively taught to speak life and quote the Word of God in prayer and in my life. At the time, I had applied for a promotion in my career with the federal government; a GS-12 position was rare, and they are difficult to achieve for some, but not me.

Oh, but my God was able. I was optimistic, enthusiastic, and determined. My desire was clear. My intention was about upward mobility; I wanted to help my mother and brother financially as well as my own son. I always talked about the promotion with excitement and expectation. I prayed about it and also saw myself driving to my work location and home office. I even had my mother praying about it.

This was my first time writing keywords on the mirror with lipstick. This particular time, I wrote big and bold "GS 12 promotion"; you could not help but see it. When anyone asked about, it was an opportunity to tell the story of my upcoming promotion that would come to pass. I not only believed, I was taking actions in my position to continue to be and do my best and finding ways to improve my performance.

A position opened up, and I applied for it; however, I was not selected. Yes, I was a little disappointed, but I encouraged myself by saying that opportunity was not intended for me; something better was on the way.

Guess what? Another opportunity did open up a short time later. Of course, I applied again, and this time was selected for an interview. I was ecstatic. I claimed it, I believed it, I saw it, and I received it. I felt extremely positive about it. I had the jitters about the interview but felt confident, despite being interviewed by three people. Afterwards, I felt the interview went great, even though I couldn't answer one of the questions. As I drove back home, I began to thank God for the opportunity to be interviewed, because in my eyes, I was closer to getting my desire. I began to thank God for everything he had done for me.

When I got home, I was still pumped and excited. I knew everything would work out for my good. For sure, I was at the highest frequency possible. While I was talking to a friend, explaining how the interview went, my manager called me to say I had gotten the promotion. All the prayers and affirmations, writing on the mirror, speaking it into the atmosphere, taking inspired action of preparation, and high emotions of appreciation, excitement, and expectation had manifested my desire.

Let's recap the steps of my manifestation, so you can learn, apply, and receive manifestations of your own:

- Be clear and specific on your desire.
- Claim it by speaking it often.
- Simply believe it is possible.
- Take actions of preparation.
- See your desire through imagination and visualization.
- Write down exactly what you desire and see for yourself.
- Express gratitude for all things in the present and the future.

Manifestation: Stay-at-Home Mom

I held that new job for a couple years, during which I grieved the death of my mother, endured the emotional anguish of two divorces, became a single mother, and coped with post-traumatic stress, anxiety, and depression after serving in Operation Enduring Freedom. As you might think, I badly needed a life makeover. The greatest part of my job, I had a flexible schedule and worked from home. One day, I took some time off to attend a Halloween activity with my son's class. I spoke with another mother, who seemed highly involved; she and her daughter came to the event in costumes she made, and she also made delicious ranch sauce and cookies.

At that moment, I had deep admiration for her life. Others might have been jealous, but I admired her whole situation; she took the time to create costumes for her and her little ones, baked homemade goodies, and had the luxury of staying home. She also had a man to care for her and her children (her husband owned his own business). All of it.

As I hurried back to home to continue working, I thought of how wonderful it would be to have a life like hers, but how could it be, when everything about my life was the opposite? My love life was in ruins, and I just went through my second divorce, but the thought of having a similar life was still wonderful.

Shortly after that, I received a mailing from Bishop T. D. Jakes that included an encouraging message, along with the opportunity to purchase one of his books. I had received many of these mailings before, but this particular one resonated deep within my spirit. The email stated that we served a big God and could ask for a God-sized blessing. Not a prayer of something that we could do for ourselves but a God-sized blessing, which only God himself could do. I immediately thought of being a stay-at-home mom; I'd be relaxed, would have more control, and could even travel at my leisure. I wrote a God-sized prayer on a Post-it note, asking to be a stay-at-home mom, to receive a lot of money, to travel, and to live life to the fullest; I also asked for unanswered prayers and placed the note in my bathroom, where I would read it every day (sometimes several times a day).

Fast-forward to a couple years later: I became a stay at mom, even before I remarried, and had financial stability. I also traveled. I still have the Post-it note; there was one sentence of a desire that I had, an unanswered prayer that may have been delayed but definitely not denied. In retrospect, I took notice of the term "or" within the unanswered prayer. I started to realize the desire was unclear; I had not given energy or a positive vibration towards that desire.

I am currently working on providing positive energy, intentions, and imagination to that desire, with expectation. I am 120 percent sure I will be writing another book to explain how it all unfolded. For I know that all things work together for my good in God's perfect timing.

Manifestation: Home and Children

After I had manifested my love interest (I felt deeply that he was my life partner and life companion) through affirmations and a vision board, I began to work on manifesting my desires of a three-thousand-square-foot home and more children. Since writing and reading in the mirror had such great results, I grabbed a tube of lipstick and wrote the following on my bedroom and bathroom mirrors:

- three-thousand-foot home
- four more kids

Every time I looked in the mirror, I saw those words, and those words were looking at me. I would reading them every time I sat on the throne. I saw them in passing, intentionally and unintentionally. They were seared into my subconscious.

Fast-forward again: I became pregnant, and shortly after, I purchased a home with a garage. I took it as a manifested desire (we expect to have more children in the near future). Once again, the lipstick worked; just kidding, it was after consistent, positive attention, energy, and, of course, much prayer to God that all my desires were manifested.

Stay Focused and Consistent

For my new desires, I still using lipstick on the mirrors, along with affirmations and other law of attraction tools. To make sure I stay focused

and take advantage of every moment, I tape note cards on my steering wheel. That way, I have no choice but to see them. I know there is no texting or reading while driving, so at every stop or pause in traffic, I speak my affirmations aloud.

I am serious about being catapulted into major success. According to my research, the average worker's commute time is twenty-six minutes; that is the perfect time to pray, decree, declare, talk to God, and praise the Lord. I know because I have done it before and still do. Sometimes, I like to play audio affirmations and listen to audiobooks. I upload my spirit, my subconscious, and my conscious mind, raising my vibration.

With my current desires, I'm using Bob Proctor's well-formulated affirmation: "I am so grateful and happy now that _____."

I like the way his affirmations incorporate appreciation, emotion, and a specific time frame (e.g., "now," which creates a higher vibration). I repeat these statements aloud with emotion, which allows them to be engraved in my subconscious.

For instance: "I am so grateful and happy now that I am a multimillionaire"; in the physical world, there is no evidence of my being a multimillionaire. But in the spiritual world, I am calling it into existence by expressing appreciation and positive emotions before being a multimillionaire is evident. As for the specific time, I say "now" instead of "someday," which is vague and in a distant future. Chapter 8 shows how to manage your emotions while you're waiting for your desires to come to fruition.

Spirituality

Below you will find scriptures regarding making a request to God from two religions. You must remember to have the audacity to dream big, always have a vision, and know that we serve a Big God who is able to do the impossible:

> Where there is no vision, the people perish: but he that keepeth the law, happy is he. (Proverbs 29:18 KJV)

> Be careful for nothing; but in everything by prayer and supplication with thanksgiving let your requests be made known unto God. (Philippians 4:6 KJV)

> Is He [not best] who responds to the desperate one when he calls upon Him. (Quran 27:62)

Exercise

Write down other desires you may have in the other major life area.

Spiritual: _____
_____
_____
_____
_____

Physical: _____
_____
_____
_____
_____

Financial: _____
_____
_____
_____
_____

Career: _____
_____
_____
_____
_____

Relationship: _____
_____
_____
_____
_____

6

Monitor Your Thoughts

According to the law of attraction, thoughts become things, which means you can create things with your thoughts. Whatever you can imagine completely, and totally believe in, you can have, do, or be. Thoughts that are given substance with fear-based feelings, such as anger, frustration, and anxiety, will become things in our physical life experience that we see as negative or bad. Thoughts given substance with love-based feelings, such as gratitude, peace, happiness, and well-being, will become things we experience as positive and good. Any thought in the mind with feelings will become a thing, whether based on love or fear.

According to *The Secret*, "What we think about, we bring about"; that explains the idea that we can attract anything we want into our lives by visualization, using affirmations, expectations, gratitude, and acting with inspiration. I know this to be true because I have tried it all and have manifested using all these 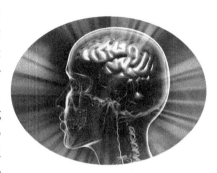 approaches. Further research states that it is important to think positive because it raises your vibration and allows you to sync with your desires.

We have about seventy thousand thoughts per day. What are your dominant thoughts? What do you think about the most within a day? Where is your focus?

If you are always thinking about how sick you are, how broke you are, or how wrong something is, you will get more of that, so try to monitor your thoughts. Find out what you're thinking about the most. Determine whether it is positive, negative, or neutral. If it is negative, simply start to add more positive thoughts. For instance, if you are sick, instead of thinking how sick you are, begin to think and speak into the atmosphere, "I am healthy now, and I am strong now."

At first, it may feel strange because you may still feel pain in your body, but continue to do think and speak positively, anyway. It might help to think of a time in your life when you were the healthiest. Also, if you have pictures, post them around your home, and know that you can be restored and return back to that physical state, with proper spiritual and mental alignment.

In Philippians 4:8, the Word of God tells us to meditate on things that are true, honest, just, pure, lovely, and good. So many people tend to overlook this scripture, especially the part about meditation. *Meditate* means "to think deeply about something." The Word of God wants us to focus on the good. This is a clear indication to me the God designed this universe and us to be able to generate power through thoughts.

God specifically encouraged his people through his Word to have positive thoughts, because he knew that it would attract more positive events, situations, and circumstances. Likewise, God knew that negative thoughts would manifest more negative events, situations, and circumstances. Remember, like attracts like. God gave us free will, so that we could make our own choices. When God created the universe, he made it unique; not even the smartest mind can fathom all of God's creation. We were given free will so we could make our own choices, according to his plan. Having free will doesn't mean we can do whatever we want without suffering the consequences; we are still responsible for the choices we make in our lives.

> Always Remember, the Choice is Yours.

So we choose our thoughts; you must decide if you want to obey God's Word on thinking positive thoughts and reap all the benefits of attracting more positive situations, events, circumstances, and people to you. Always remember, the choice is yours.

There are lot of thoughts that may be going through your mind. One way to calm you mind is through meditation and breathing methods. It's also good to write down your dominant thoughts. Analyze them and adjust your thoughts as appropriate. Practice observing your thoughts as they pass by. The Bible even says to be transformed by the renewal of your mind, which mean reprogramming your mind for positive change. Writing out positive affirmations is also beneficial.

Another way to calm your mind is to focus on the present. Focus on the now. Leave the past in the past, focus on the now, and look forward to the future, with hope for all things to come. The Bible even mentions forgetting what lies behind and reaching for those things before you, to press towards your goals (Philippians 3:13). The Word of God goes on to encourage contentment, meaning you must learn to be happy in whatever state you are in, wherever you are (Philippians 4:11).

My Experience with Thoughts

I'd like to share one of my recent events with the power of thoughts. After I moved to Alabama from Michigan, I was blessed to meet my life partner and gave birth to another bundle of joy; we were in search of a church home for our family. Since I came from a big family who all went to various churches, we would visit a church for months at a time, trying to decide which one was the best fit for us. Many times, George and I would discuss how great it would be for us to find a church where our children could go to Sunday school, vacation Bible school, youth meetings, and church outings. We talked about our own experiences growing up and how it built a great foundation within us. We spoke of appreciating our parents for making us go to church. I, myself, felt appreciation for other adults, including Minister Darneal Marble, my eldest aunt, who faithfully worked with us, as well as those who generously sponsored my trips.

You see, my mother was a single parent, and we grew up on welfare; she could not afford to send me on church outings. However, I was able to go because of someone's giving heart; in addition, the Greater Harvest Baptist Church youth group raised funds for others to attend. I have many great memories of attending various youth conferences, parks, and other events I would not have been able to go to. So I will be forever grateful to those who gave their time, energy, and money. I have gone a step further to pay it forward to others. As you can understand, we wanted our children to have those same great memories.

Manifestation: Church Home and Church Family

While we discussed, contemplated, and reminisced, we were generating high vibrations of gratitude and love. We even talked about how great it would be if we, as adults, could also be active in the church. This went on for some time, Sunday after Sunday, for about year and half, without deciding on a church to join. We did not want to rush the process.

One day, we were running extremely late for church; we had to leave early because the church we were visiting at time was about half an hour away. So George and I went back and forth on who would decide where to go. Well, he decided on a church that we saw while driving down the street, months earlier. This church was five minutes away from us. It was like heaven opened up for us, we instantly knew but we continue to visit to make sure it was a great fit. Let me tell you, it was a great fit.

We joined months later. I began to learn I was related to a lot of people or they knew my family. My kids instantly made close friends. We received a lot of love and care. We all became active in Sunday school, Bible study, and Vacation Bible School. My oldest became an usher, partook in holiday activities, sang in the choir, and was active in other young activities. My youngest became everyone's baby, meaning everyone loved on him and kept him during church. As work permitted, my husband took part in activities and also drove the church bus. I joined the choir and helped with vacation Bible school, the women's social circle, and the women's retreat. Our church home is now True Deliverance Holiness Church. It was heaven sent. Remember all these discussions, thoughts, the feeling of gratitude, and trip down memory lane feelings were all positive vibrations being sent into the atmosphere or universe. Well, God began to orchestrate everything to bring us our desires. It all started with thoughts and feelings (a very powerful combination) for manifestation.

My Musical Inspiration

"Your Righteous Mind" is a 2011 song by Donald Lawrence and Co., featuring Dorinda Clark Cole, which encouraged me to monitor my activities due to the effects on my mind and decide why God wanted us to think of things that were positive, as mentioned in Philippians 4:8. For the entire set of lyrics, check out the following website: www.azlyrics.com/lyrics/donaldlawrence/yrmyourrighteousmind.html

If ye be risen, risen, risen in Christ in Christ.
Set your affections, affections, on the things of the kingdom.

See your righteous mind is a faith mind.
Your righteous mind is a miracle mind.
Jesus came and He did it.
Your righteous mind.
Time for you to get with it.
Your righteous mind.

Spirituality

Here are some verses that stress the importance of your thoughts:

Finally, brethren, whatsoever things are true, whatsoever things are honest, whatsoever things are just, whatsoever things are pure, whatsoever things are lovely, whatsoever things are of good report; if there be any virtue, and if there be any praise, think on these things. (Philippians 4:8 KJV)

As a man thinketh in his heart, so he is. (Proverbs 23:7 KJV)

With our thoughts, we make the world. (Buddha)

All that we are is the result of what we have thought. The mind is everything. What we think we become. (Buddha)

Exercise

What are your dominant thoughts in the major life areas? Are they positive or negative? If negative, write down how you can alter those thoughts to something positive. Or if neutral, write an improved statement.

Example: Relationship (negative): There are no more good women (or men) out there.

Correct: The right one for me is on the way now.

Spiritual: _____
_____
_____
_____

Physical: _____
_____
_____
_____

Financial: _____
_____
_____
_____

Career: _____
_____
_____
_____

Relationship: _____
_____
_____
_____

7

Imagine If ...

magination is a powerful force, according to my research, but I must admit, I have not previously used this strategy until now. I tend to use my imagination by default, meaning I do it automatically, without even realizing it. When I admired the stay-at-home mom's ability to spend quality time with her children at school functions without having to balance work and home life, I imagine myself in that position. In fact, that came to pass after some major changes in my life. When I do see myself doing something in my mind, I actually do it in the natural realm.

Many researchers, scientists, and leaders believe that imagination is a creative, miraculous, powerful force. If imagination is so important and powerful, why do young children get in trouble for daydreaming? Adults are told daydreaming is unproductive and a waste of time; we're discouraged from doing it. Therefore, we become conditioned in a negative way about daydreaming as children.

When I first started out intentionally imagining my current desires, I felt like I had to remove the rust from that part of my brain to get it moving again. I was out of practice and felt awkward, but I needed to actively get my imagination functioning properly. I learned that it's important to use your imagination when manifesting things through the law of attraction.

During my research, I learned about visualization. Rev. Ike Williams, who regularly gives visualization treatments to his congregation, once spoke of using the stage of imagination in your mind. He consistently stressed the importance of using your imagination for things that you desire. I initially believed that visualization and imagination were used interchangeably; however, I found the following on Wikipedia: "Imagination: the capacity to produce images, ideas and sensations in the mind without any immediate input of the senses. Visualization: the act or an instance of visualizing; (Psychology) a procedure involving focusing on positive mental images to achieve a particular goal."

I decided that they were used interchangeably but were not always the same. To make it simple, my understanding is that imagination is a mental image with sensory input, and visualization is a mental image without the use of senses; there's more attention to detail, and the image can be viewed at all possible angles. No matter the correct definition, it is very powerful process, especially when it engages your senses. One must live in that image for it to become reality.

My Experience with Imagination

For this section, I will be using the words *visualization* and *imagination* interchangeably. I have not yet manifested any experiences using visualization methods. Take notice I said "yet," meaning I expect marvelous experiences any day now. I know the desires I visualize will come to pass in God's perfect timing. For I know that the best is yet to come. I will explain how I plan to incorporate these skills into my daily life. Visualization is a tool used by elite athletes, celebrities, and other successful individuals to achieve their goals and dreams. Successful visualization takes practice.

Here are the steps I am implementing:

1. I begin with a positive state of mind, such as gratitude or love.
2. I include all five senses: smell, taste, touch, hearing, and sight; I focus on all details and actively participate in the visualization.
3. I put a lot of emotion into it.
4. I practice daily for ten to twenty minutes.

I have manifested several things, people, and places using vision boards. I first become aware of vision boards when I started researching the law of attraction. I learned that a vision board is a tool used to help clarify, concentrate, and maintain focus on a specific life goal. You display various images on a board that you want to be, do, or have in your life. The purpose of a vision board is to help you identify your vision, clarify your daily affirmations, and keep your attention on your intentions. A vision board is a powerful visualization tool that can inspire you. I have heard many stories of how celebrities have used vision boards.

To create your own vision board, you'll need a foam or canvas board, a stack of old magazines or photos that inspire you, scissors, markers, glue, and tape. Before starting, set the atmosphere for relaxation and concentration. Cut out or print images that represent the life you want to live. For example, if you want to be a home decorator, you might clip or print photos of interior designs you like. Begin to arrange and attach the photos as you desire. Place the vision board where you'll see it every day and feel inspired.

I used Oprah's dream board from her website; I could print this vision board for easy access. On my first vision board, I included images that relate to the following areas:

- my own life partner or companion
- my own loving family and kids
- a closer relationship with God
- better health
- more travel and more fun
- wealth and prosperity
- a dream home become a reality
- begin a new career or start my own business

I have a new vision board that I made out of extra-large paper. For each life area, I have an image with an affirmation statement with related scripture. The areas include

- family,
- travel,
- wealth and prosperity,
- fitness, and
- charity.

It has already start to unfold and manifest in our lives. I look forward to displaying to the world my final vision once it's fully manifested, which I expect will happen very soon.

Props

While vision boards are great, props maybe even better because they are things that allow you to touch, feel, and see; they are more realistic and invoke emotions and vibrations while you use your imagination and hold on to the item. I bought a customized trophy so I can touch how it would be when I actually received an award. I locate it where I can always see it consciously and subconsciously.

I have superimposed my face onto someone else's body, so that I can really see myself within that image. For my latest vision board, I wanted to be super creative while being very specific. I created an image with myself holding a huge sweepstakes check, surrounded by my family. I place the printed poster on my ceiling so I'd see the image as I was drifting off to sleep and when I woke up. You may not want to use the ceiling as I did, but you should position your vision board where you will see it the most.

It may seem crazy to some, but it's not. It's actually a fantastic idea, especially when you read about people who've done it and manifested great results. One needs to really live in that moment through your imagination for it to become reality. I think this is the best way to do, especially if you're used to activating your imaginative skills.

I got the idea for superimposed images from Terry Foy Savelle. I came across her when I was researching why law of attraction methods were not being implemented by church folks, especially when it is the Word of God in action. It is biblical. I know a lot of people who know the Word of God but do not know how to properly apply it in their everyday lives. So they do not receive the full benefits of what God has intended for them, whereas people who are nonspiritual are manifesting left and right.

Creating a vision board with superimposed pictures may seem too extreme for you; you should do what works for you. Different people have different levels of imagination. This strategy makes it more believable. Remember, the point is to make it believable for you. You must really see yourself in it. It depends on how serious you are about manifesting your desires. For my new vision board, I'm using more advanced imaginative skills by Neville Goddard, in which I use all my God-given senses to really live in the moment I desire. For some people, the use of imaginative methods is simple.

As children, we are encouraged to use our imagination, but then at some point, we get so serious, dull, and logical in our life, trying to make sure we get an education as a means to get a career, only to become even more serious. The childlike spirit that made it easy to imagine diminished, but with practice and guidance, it can be rediscovered.

Mind Movies

I first learned about mind movies while learning about the law of attraction. Mind movies can transform a boring vision board into a fun board filled with positive affirmations, inspiring videos, and motivating music. Natalie Ledwell sells multiple products pertaining to mind movies; she's helped millions of people around the world to be empowered to reach their goals. I made my own mind movie using inspirational images and songs about love, family, and home. I uploaded my information onto a movie-making app that allowed me to create a five-minute video, which I frequently watched and ultimately manifested.

A combination of written and spoken affirmations, vision boards, and mind movies were revealed while writing this book, and last but not least, fervent prayer allowed me to manifest my dreams. That's a great way to ingrain the images and the feelings within your subconscious mind. My research into the law of attraction led me to a different type of mind movie inspired by Peter Adams; he won the Ironman race after watching a movie of the race hundreds of times, until he could imagine it was him. That requires great dedication and commitment. This is an approach that I would like to implement for myself.

My Musical Inspiration

The best song that relates to this chapter on imagination is Tamela Mann's *I Can Only Imagine* (2013); she sings about her imagination of seeing Jesus and what she would do before the King. She sings about what it would be like in his presence. Using her imagination, she visualized whether she would dance, be still, fall to her knees, sing hallelujah, or stay silent. This is a lovely song to bask in the glory of the Lord, no matter what you decide to do; it's majestic. In a similar matter of using imagination, you could change options, angels, or any details of the outcome. For the lyrics to this beautiful song, please visit www.azlyrics.com/lyrics/tamelamann/icanonlyimagine.html

I can only imagine.
Can you imagine, just standing before the King?
Ooooh.
I can only imagine
what it would be like
when I walk by your side.
I can only imagine, yeah,
what my eyes would see,
when your face is before me.

Spirituality

Even the Lord himself knows the power of imagination, especially since he created us and the power:

And the LORD said, Behold, the people [are] one, and
they have all one language; and this they begin to do:
and now nothing will be restrained from them, which
they have imagined to do. (Genesis 11:6 KJV)

Although God gave us the power of imagination, it is still no match for his infinite divine power and knowledge:

That is what the Scriptures mean when they say, "No eye has seen, no ear has heard, and no mind has imagined what God has prepared for those who love him." (1 Corinthians 2:9 NLT)

God is able to multiply our blessings, if we realize and access our divine power through imagination and speaking:

Now unto him that is able to do exceeding abundantly above all that we ask or think, according to the power that worketh in us. (Ephesians 3:20 KJV)

Exercise

Have the audacity to allow your imagination to run wild. Dream, think, and write an enormous imagination in the five major areas of life. There are no limits; have at it. Example: Relationship (negative): There are no more good women (or men) out there.

Spiritual: _____
_____
_____
_____
_____

Physical: _____
_____
_____
_____
_____

Financial: _____
_____
_____
_____
_____

Career: _____
_____
_____
_____
_____

Relationship: _____
_____
_____
_____

8

In Your Feelings

Feelings and emotions are important in the law of attraction. While the two words are used interchangeably, there is a difference. Feelings are low-key but sustainable. Emotions are intense but temporary. Since they are two sides of the same coin and highly interconnected, for the sake of this chapter, I will discuss them together. It is imperative to be conscious of your feelings and emotions, considering that they are direct indications of your vibrations and the frequency you are on. Feelings and emotions are both energy in motion. Whatever energy you put out is the same energy that will be mirrored back to you. I especially like the illustrated examples in Rhoda Byrne's *The Secret*. If you think of your emotions, which is a direct link to your vibrations or frequency, like an echo, a boomerang, or a copying machine, it will help you understand that what you put out in terms of feelings, imagination, words, and thoughts is what you get back in return.

Let's continue the copying machine illustration, as most people have experience with it. If you go to a printing store and make copies of party invitations, if you follow the copy machine instructions, you expect to get an exact replica of the original. Correct? Nothing more, and nothing less. In the same way, if you have the emotional state of joy, a copy of your vibrational signals are sent into the universe, returning back to you people, circumstances, and situations that will bring you more joy. The opposite is also true; if you are in the emotional state of sadness, a copy of your vibrational signals are sent into the universe, returning to you people, circumstances, and situations in that frequency, thus causing more sadness. It will be a continuous cycle, until you decide to switch to a different frequency, meaning a different emotion or feeling.

You might think that you have no control over your emotions. On the contrary, you do have some control. You should become aware of how you feel because as previously stated, it is a valuable indicator of your vibrational frequency and whether you allow the fulfillment of your

> **Choose wisely:**
> **Feelings and emotions affect the outcome of your life.**

desires or not. For instance, Esther and Jerry Hicks's fuel gauge analogy interprets emotions as an indicator. It is a very relatable illustration that should resonate for most people. As we know, all cars require fuel to operate. Cars have a fuel gauge, which reflects the amount of gas in the tank. If the fuel gauge reads empty, you don't blame the indicator but acknowledge the information and add more gas to the tank.

This same issue applies to your emotions. As you become aware of your emotional state, which is your fuel gauge, you should take immediate action. If you are in a low-vibrational emotion, start by adding better thoughts, which in turn will improve your emotions. Yes, that means your fuel is your positive thoughts. Your thoughts affect your emotions; emotions indicate your vibration and energy. Choose wisely: Feelings and emotions affect the outcome of your life.

So how do you become aware and analyze your feelings and emotions? This is especially hard if your emotions and feelings change from one moment to the next. Well, it takes patience and practice, as well as awareness tools such as meditation, yoga, and journaling, to name a few. It is important to assess your current state of mind and see how it relates to your life right now. Then you become self-aware of your current emotional state and thought patterns. Positive experiences come into your life when you change your thoughts, which are a result of your feelings and emotions; this must be done from the root: the subconscious layer of the mind. Meditation helps establish crystal-clear thinking and offers the following benefits:

- frees the mind from self-doubt and negative internal chatter
- improves concentration and strengthens the mind
- brings more peace of mind
- increases creativity
- releases fear
- reduces anxiety
- generates optimism, self-esteem, confidence, and motivation

With all of these benefits, you will surely have positive vibrations, thus easily manifesting your desires.

Thoughts create feelings.

⬇

Feelings create behavior.

⬇

Behavior reinforces thoughts.

Another awareness tool is journaling, which has numerous benefits and helps you deal with your daily emotions. Journaling is simply writing down your thoughts and feelings to understand them clearly. It can provide a healthy outlet where you can safely express yourself. This helpful tool can help reduce anxiety and stress. If you struggle with depression or any other mental health issue, journaling helps you gain better control of your emotions, which improves your mental health. Journaling is therapeutic and can be used as reflective writing; you or a therapist can analyze your thoughts and feelings in order to make the proper adjustments and raise your vibrational frequency.

I strongly encourage you to purchase a journal or a simple notebook and start to journal, every day or once a week or whenever you are overwhelmed by your emotions. The ideas is to write down your feelings, thoughts, and experiences; monitor your

emotions and practice elevating them by adding better feelings and thoughts and memories. In the next section, we will discuss ways to raise your vibration.

Exhibit 8. Better-Feeling Thoughts Examples

Law of Attraction	The Bible
It's on its way.	I am blessed and highly favored.
Now it's getting even better.	All things work together for my good.
The process has begun.	
I am worthy.	God is my Redeemer.
I am so loved.	Go is my healer.
I can choose my thoughts and emotions, and change my world.	God is my provider.
	He is my deliverer.
I enjoy my life.	He supplies all my needs.

Raising Your Vibrational Frequency

Esther and Jerry Hicks made a valid point: Adding better feelings thoughts improves your emotional state and increases your vibrational frequency. There are many other ways to raise your vibration. I have listed ten activities that have helped me. I, too, take advantage of the benefits of meditation and journaling; however, there are other ways that can assist you. Remember, the law of attraction, which is the application of the Word of God, is a lifestyle.

1. Show Gratitude.

Gratitude is the quickest and most effective way to raise your vibration. If you are in a negative spirit or frequency, simply stop everything and look around yourself, no matter where you are. Say to yourself, "I am grateful ...," and simply fill in the blank. While it might seem too simplistic, it does work and is very powerful. Just try it. You'll start to feel better. For example:

- I am grateful for the roof over my head.
- I am grateful for my eyesight, hearing, and mobility.
- I am grateful for my family, church family, and friends.

2. Repeat Affirmations.

Affirmations are positive statements that you repeat over and over; spoken with high emotions and conviction, they imprint on your subconscious mind, raise your vibration, and increase your energy and power. The idea is to find or create empowering affirmations that resonate within your heart. While you can read affirmations anywhere, it's beneficial to read them in front of a mirror, symbolizing you speaking life into yourself. Once you start to use affirmations, you may feel odd or as though you are lying, but you are not. You are speaking in faith, calling those that are not, as though they were. In otherwise, speaking life into existence. Calling forth those things that are in the spirit realm into the physical realm.

3. Give to Others.

Give something to someone without expecting anything in return. Buy someone coffee. Donate to a charitable organization. Giving shifts your mentality from "not having enough" to "having more than enough to give to others." This will invoke the feeling of abundance, which is a high-vibrational frequency.

4. Listen to Music.

Music can raise your vibration to the highest frequency, fast. This is one of my favorite ways to shift to positive energy. Be sure to select music with powerful positive words; such songs can make you feel great. Choose a song with upbeat tones and higher pitch to achieve higher vibration.

5. Declutter Your Space.

Clutter in your work or living space signifies energetic clutter, inside and out. It represents stuck, stagnant energy and can prevent you from creating the life you desire. Removing the clutter releases your energy;

it flows freely around you and your space, which in turn raises your frequency.

6. Take a Relaxing Bath.

Each passing year, we're expected to go faster and faster, thus causing us to always be in a rush. This even includes our self-care. It's safe to say that most people take a shower as part of their daily routine, but they are often in a rush, which unknowingly creates more stress in their life and lowers their vibrational frequency.

Baths actually have medicinal benefits; they focus on psychological relaxation and allow you to target specific conditions. It is also a part of self-love, which is a great way to raise your vibration by loving on yourself. In my opinion, you can't expect someone else to love you when you don't love yourself. We must set the tone and the standard on what we expect to receive from others. What you give to yourself is what you can expect from others. Did you know that your body is a temple of God? Your body, which includes your mind, was bought with the price of God's only begotten Son, Jesus, so glorify God in your body in every aspect.

7. Dance or Exercise.

The human body is made to move. When your body moves, your energy also moves, releasing endorphins and making you feel happier, thus drawing more happy experiences to you. You could take a walk in nature or do some other enjoyable activity, such as stretching, yoga, bicycling, or wrestling; the options are endless. Movement helps oxygenate the body and brain, cleanses your lymph system, and produces energy that increases higher vibrations to manifest your desires.

8. Vibrational Acquaintances.

You might be thinking that certain areas of your life are not affected by your emotions; however, you would be wrong. You might think that the people you interact with on a regular basis have no effect on you at all. Oh, but they do. Family and friends can, in fact, lower your frequency; I'm sure you know this for yourself. Do you avoid answering the phone when a certain family member or friend calls? Do you feel emotionally drained after spending time with someone? Do you have a relationship with someone who is always taking without giving?

If you stated yes to any of these, then you know these people are lowering your vibrational frequency; remember, your emotional state is a direct indicator of your frequency level. These people are energy vampires, sucking your vital life force and self-esteem away; interacting with them brings you down and makes you feel worse than before. My advice is to minimize contact and avoid if possible; however, if they are family, you have no other option but to interact. Just pray ahead of time for protection as well as afterwards to release any negative energy. You may also practice self-healing techniques such as meditation and visualization, or do something that makes you happy.

9. Living Space.

Places and things hold energy, especially homes. A house is not just purely physical matter; it also vibrates with invisible energy. Since you are in your home a lot, whatever is present will affect your vibration. That is why it's good to bless your home or do a spirit cleansing; you should also align your beliefs, desires, and vibrational frequency with your home's prayers, paintings, photographs, statues, books, and plants; the color of the walls can also be changed to match your spirit. Some people use feng shui techniques to design their home. All objects possess energy, and arranging your furniture in a certain way can help the flow of energy and bring luck, wealth, and opportunity to your home.

10. Reduce Low-Vibrational Frequencies.

The media is accessible today via a number of electronic devices, such as cell phones, tablets, TVs, and computers, to name a few. While these items can be used for good, there is definitely an equal opportunity for a constant stream of negativity coming directly to you and your home. Thus, you need to monitor the negativity, reduce the drama, and eliminate altogether anything with violence. This extends to friends and extended family who are always on a low-vibrational frequency, such as gossiping, criticizing, complaining, fault-finding, shaming, and son on; those negative frequencies can affect your vibrations.

Emotional Guidance

Since I am a visual person, the Emotional Guidance Scale has been a godsend. Abraham-Hicks' Emotional Guidance Scale (2004) is presented in exhibit 8.1; it consists of a series of emotions. You can map where you are emotionally, now and where you'd like to be. Since the only way to manifest something positive is to feel good first, it's essential to be conscious of your frequency. Once you acknowledge and understand your emotions and feelings, you'll be one step closer to manifesting the life you desire.

As previously stated, your emotions are a direct indicator of your vibrational frequency at any given moment. One can even say your emotions are like a compass that requires you to be always pointed north (north being the highest frequency you can achieve). Thanks to Abraham-Hicks's map, we can visually recognize our current level and see what the next level is to achieve. Remember, feeling better could be achieved by adding better feelings thoughts or any other tools that you prefer.

So what is this emotional guidance scale? It illustrates twenty-two of our most commonly felt emotions, from the highest, being joy, appreciation, empowerment, freedom, and love, to the lowest, being fear, grief, depression, despair, and powerlessness. Next, you identify the emotion you are feeling at that moment. After you name it, own it, and accept it, you must decide it is time to let go of that emotion and increase your emotional frequency level by feeling better, with the right positive thoughts.

Examples

Let's look at my life and emotions during writing this book. Hopefully, you will see an accurate illustration. At this moment, I am listening to old-school R&B hits as well as concentration binaural beats. I am definitely in the flow of writing. As I previously mentioned, I use music, especially gospel music, to encourage myself and lift up my spirits; while writing, these old classics keep me in a great writing mood. In all fairness, I also completed my morning routine of prayer, meditation, affirmations, visualizations, reading my Bible, and journaling. Using all these tools is like drinking a gallon of the strongest coffee first thing in the morning. My vibration is through the roof.

As we assess my current emotional state, taking into consideration the foundation of law of attraction tools and good-feeling music, I am feeling "positive expectation" and "enthusiasm" (as listed in exhibit 8.1, emotion 4 and 3, respectively). It is better to choose one, but I am between the two at this moment. Now that I have identified the emotions of enthusiasm and positive expectation, I have named, owned, and accepted them and let them know there is room for improvement in my frequency and energy. Next, I need to add the right kind of thoughts (see exhibit 8), and I already have some easily available, for I already have positive expectations of the following:

- I expect my book to be a *New York Times* best-seller.
- This book is a great piece of work.
- My miraculous desires are on the way to me now.
- The best is upon me now.

Since I am listening to music, I simply switch to high-vibrational songs, "Feeling Good" by Nina Simone, and "Happy" by Pharrell. I close my eyes, allowing the melody and lyrics to elevate my energy to joy, appreciation, empowerment, freedom, love (as indicated in exhibit 8.1). I actually feel like dancing, but I'm at my local library; I'll wait until I get home. I can actually feel the energy surge throughout my body. My expectations and better-feeling thoughts are sure to manifest.

Keep trying to achieve the best emotion possible. Remember,

everything is energy, and everything has a vibrational frequency. That includes your feelings, which resonate at a particular frequency. Whether your feelings or emotions are high or low, that means high or low vibrations are always matched back to you, respectively. Vibrational frequencies are seen on a scale from high to low (see exhibit 8.1 for a similar chart).

Exhibit 8.1. The Emotional Guidance Scale

1. Joy/Appreciation/Empowerment/Freedom/Love
2. Passion
3. Enthusiasm/Eagerness/Happiness
4. Positive Expectation/Belief
5. Optimism
6. Hopefulness
7. Contentment
8. Boredom
9. Pessimism
10. Frustration/Irritation/Impatience
11. Overwhelmed
12. Disappointment
13. Doubt
14. Worry
15. Blame
16. Discouragement
17. Anger
18. Revenge
19. Hatred/Rage
20. Jealousy
21. Insecurity/Guilt/Unworthiness
22. Fear/Grief/Depression/Despair/Powerlessness

Emotional Type

Knowing the type of person you are emotionally helps you see how you perceive the world and how it affects you; you can use this information to create your highest vibrational emotions. This scale was developed by Dr. Judith Orloff (2011), who explains how there are four main emotional types: the Intellectual, the Empath, the Rock, and the Gusher, all of which she observed in her psychiatric practice. She believes that knowing your type can provide insight into how you interact with others and also will help you master your emotions properly. Rather than ignore or avoid your feelings, you learn to create a healthy balance. I created a chart below of Dr. Orloff's emotional types. After you determine your emotional type, see her suggested tips for your emotional type. Between Abraham-Hicks's scale and Dr. Orloff's assessment, you will most definitely be conscious of your internal power source (your emotion) and be able to set it to highest level frequency possible for manifesting the life your heart truly desires and deserves. Let's get started:

Exercise

What Is Your Emotional Type?			
Type 1: The Intellectual	Type 2: The Empath	Type 3: The Rock	Type 4: The Gusher
Intense Thinker	*Emotional Sponge*	*Strong and Silent Type*	*Attuned to Emotions*
❑ Bright ❑ Articulate ❑ Analytical ❑ Intellectually oriented ❑ Rational ❑ Calm in heated situation ❑ Struggle with emotions	❑ Highly sensitive ❑ Loving and supportive ❑ Naturally giving ❑ Spiritually attuned ❑ A good listener ❑ Feels everything	❑ Emotionally strong for self and others ❑ Practical ❑ Able to stay cool in a crisis ❑ Nonjudgmental ❑ Dependable ❑ Stable ❑ Hard time expressing emotions	❑ Aware of your emotions ❑ Shares emotions often ❑ Spontaneous ❑ Direct ❑ Authentic

According to Dr. Orloff, each emotional type has a downside that I'd like to address as it relates to this chapter. By being self-aware of your qualities, along with the pros and cons of your emotional type, you'll learn how to implement self-control. Below I have listed Dr. Orloff's Balance Prescription under the respective emotional types. If you consistently and properly implement what the doctor has ordered, you will be emotionally healthy in no time and maintain the highest emotional frequency possible. If you'd like more details on emotions as delivered by Dr. Orloff, I highly recommend her book *Emotional Freedom*. In the meantime, let's get started on following the doctor's orders.

Doctor's Orders

Emotional Type 1: The Intellectual

You have difficulty connecting with your feelings and those of others, so it's important to spend more time in your physical and sensual self; try breathing techniques, vigorous exercise, and practicing empathizing with other people's feelings. I definitely agree with this prescription, especially since I would administer a huge dose to my father, who seems to be a giant brain with legs and arms. I could write an entire book on the importance of having a heart along with your brain; I know how lacking love, care, and compassion can leave you emotionally bankrupt. By lacking these qualities, an intellectual would be more likely to make decisions based on logic and disregard the feelings of others.

Emotional Type 2: The Empath

Dr. Orloff recommends using positive self-talk and logic to get grounded. Be sure to frequent allow time to be quiet and meditate. Protect yourself by setting clear limits and boundaries as well as taking space for yourself; learn to walk away and say no. I concur with this prescription, because I, too, am an empath, and these recommendations have helped me tremendously. By protecting myself from drama and energy vampires, I have been able to preserve my energy for much more beneficial and productive activities, such as writing this book, creating a motivational series, and opening a business. Remember, the key is to be consistent, and you will definitely see results.

Emotional Type 3: The Rock

Dr. Orloff's prescription states that you should practice activities that are spontaneous and choose one feeling a day to express. She also stated that you should initiate conversations that are emotional. I concur with her suggestions because I have firsthand knowledge of dealing the Rock, because I am married to one. Thank goodness I saw the best in him; if

I hadn't used my strong sense of intuition, I could have let this angel go. In the beginning of our relationship, I nagged, begged, and ever cried for him to open up with his emotions. He is still the Rock I met, but I chose to appreciate all the qualities he exhibited; he was strong, stable, and supportive. And although he was silent, he was still very sweet. Rather than using a lot of words, he showed his emotions in action by always being there; he made several sweet gestures such as sending flowers every few weeks and expressed his emotions in messages, cards, and texts. I'll take it.

Emotional Type: The Gusher

Dr. Orloff prescribes that you, too, use positive self-talk as well as practice activities that support and strengthen your self-sufficiency. She goes on to recommend that you give yourself credit and learn to forgive yourself. Again, I concur with these recommendations; I know several gushers who have great qualities, but they'll be even greater when they know their own worth. They must know that just as they forgive others, they should forgive themselves for the shortcomings and mistakes they've made.

My Experience with Emotions

According to Dr. Orloff's analysis, I am considered an Empath. I first became aware of this emotional typing through my personal development. After doing my own research, I became more aware of who I am. I learned that my emotions determine how I view people, situations, and circumstances. I must say it would have been awesome to have this information years ago, as I matured emotionally. I am sure there are many others who lack this knowledge, and they fail miserably at assessing themselves. There is definitely power in knowledge. I can honestly say in my younger years, I was a very emotional person. I loved hard, and if love failed, I would be devastated. When I got upset, I would become enraged. As I grew wiser, I learned self-control. I am still a work in progress, but thank God, I'm better than I used to be. I used to resent the emotions the Lord gave me because I was so sensitive; I felt everything. That was because I did not fully understand it was a God-given tool and not a curse.

As I became wiser, I learned that your feelings are like a compass, allowing you to determine which level you vibrate on. Like a physical compass, if you are going in the wrong direction, this knowledge allows you to make the proper adjustments and get on the right track. The right track is in a high-vibrational frequency for the purpose of manifesting your desires and feeling about your life. In my upbringing, no one addressed emotions; in addition, my military experience taught me to suck it up and drive on. It was the norm in my family to hide your feelings and sweep your emotions under the rug; everyone pretended the mountain of emotions covered by a rug did not exist, and they'd deny it if anyone had the audacity to bring it up. As a result of this façade, I watched as stress and depression broke down my own mother, and that was later repeated in my own life, until I decided I needed help.

In today's society, there is such as negative stigma regarding seeking mental health, especially in the black community and among veterans. Seeking mental health is perceived as a weakness; it's seen as a sign of being crazy, when in fact it is a cowardly or prideful move *not* to get help. Instead, people believe they can just pray about it and go about their day, despite the mental anguish blasting out the seams of your life. Did God not give us doctors and medical advancements? Does that not include psychologists and psychiatrists? They are doctors of the mind.

You wouldn't walk around on a broken leg, only offering up prayers for healing. No, you would seek medical attention. So why is it that when people's mental health is deteriorating, they deny it or delay seeking assistance? Why do they only pray about it? Doesn't the Word of God say that faith without works is dead? That means you can believe all day, but if you take no action, then nothing will happen. It is normal for me to witness people seeking help only after something terrible has happened, like someone gets hurt. Were the signs of mental illness not visible before, or did everyone simply ignore the issues? I encourage you to speak with a therapist or close friend if you see or feel signs of emotional distress; please address them as soon as possible.

My Musical Inspiration

While I have used mostly gospel songs to help me raise my vibration or praise God through difficult situations or events, "Happy," an R&B song by Pharrell, is just as great, positive, and uplifting. It can instantly elevate your feelings; its upbeat and positive lyrics will quickly have you grooving into a higher vibration. The song is about just being happy and there is nothing anyone can do about it. Even if bad things happen, the singer remains unbothered and stays happy. This is definitely a song with a great powerful message that everyone can learn and pattern themselves from.

I used this next song in my first mind movie as I visualized a loving, caring family of my own, which I gladly possess today. "Feeling Good," which was recorded by Nina Simone in 1965, makes you feel good immediately, with lyrics that invoke your imagination to see the birds in the sunny sky and even pleasant memories of lovely breezes. This beautiful old song is still able to summons cheerful recollections in your life with its verses about flowing rivers, sights of dawn, a dragonfly out in the sun, butterflies, and the stars. When she sings, "It's a new day," it can make the saddest person crack a hopeful smile. This song truly feels good. As previously stated, it is very important to pay attention to lyrics, especially in today's society, where too many artists sing about violence, hurt, pain, drugs, sex, alcohol, and death. It is enough to make the happiest person bottom out on the emotional frequency scale.

Spirituality

Emotions play an important role in our lives, including our spiritual being. We realize that emotions can be so complex that they cloud our thinking, to the point we do things we should not or would not normally do. Emotions and feelings are complex, which can be confusing, uncertain, as well as dangerous. This is when spiritual guidance in religious life is important.

Each religion has its own sacred book, such as the Bible; spiritual leaders base their teachings on these books to educate and guide their followers, stressing the importance of controlling their emotions as well as connecting to God (or their higher divine power) for guidance and help. In the Bible, the apostle Paul tells the people of God to live peaceably with others, as much as possible, because he himself knew it could be a difficult task. Apostle Peter speaks of having knowledge with self-control. The Word of God encourages people to have faith, hope, and love, with the greatest of these being love. Below are a few religious verses to reflect the importance of emotions.

Apostle Paul encourages us not to worry, rather manage your anxiety by praying and petitioning God, while also giving thanks to him; ask for your desires, and then you will experience peace that no one else could understand.

> Do not be anxious about anything, but in everything by prayer and supplication with thanksgiving let your requests be made known to God. And the peace of God, which surpasses all understanding, will guard your hearts and your minds in Christ Jesus. (Philippian 4:6–7 ESV)

See, even Jesus wants you to be happy; just knowing this makes me feel secure and provides peace of mind. I hope it does the same for you.

> These things I have spoken unto you, that in me ye might have peace. In the world ye shall have tribulation: but be of good cheer; I have overcome. (John 16:33 KJV)

Here are some great quotes from leaders of different religions that share similar principles regarding feelings and emotions:

> Feelings are just visitors. Let them come and go. (Mooji)

> Everything is temporary: emotions, thoughts, people, and their scenery. Do not become attached, just flow with it. (Buddha)

9

"Act as If …"

The "Act as If …" technique is very powerful. You may know the saying "Faith without works is dead." Well, it's not just a saying; it is, in fact, a biblical scripture meaning one cannot only believe but must

also put in some work, or nothing will happen. This verse is aligned with the law of attraction's principle of taking inspired action. Inspired action is when you receive an idea, impulse, or urge to do something, especially when your faith level is high and you know without a doubt that your desire will be given to you, and you feel great about it.

I implemented this approach without even realizing it was part of the law of attraction. The "Act As If …" action demonstrates that you have an expectation. It's just like praising God in advance for what he's about to do. While others are trying to get ready, you are revealing to God that you are ready now; you truly believe you will get what you asked him for, and you are grateful now. You must believe to the point that you know it's going to happen; if you know something is going to happen, you take the proper actions to prepare. You must act as if you have it already.

This may be a difficult concept; some people have to see it before they believe it. But if you have faith in the Word of God and know how the law of attraction works, you'll know that you must believe it before you can see it. The law of attraction is not just about good feelings and good thoughts; it requires action to get the energy moving so you manifest your desires.

Examples

If you want a job or a new career, here are some examples of acting out your desire now:

- If you're looking for a new job, begin to dress for the job you want now.
- Imagine wearing the uniform or outfit your new job will require.
- Open a bank account to deposit your new paycheck.
- Update your resume and reference list. Practice answering interview questions in the mirror, or have a friend pose potential questions and critique your answers.

My Experience with Action

This is how I implemented this technique: My husband quit his job with the state and took a leap of faith to launch our trucking business. I encouraged him to purchase the items he needed now, such as boots and gloves. To my surprise, he had already started doing it. I got him a placard that had his name and title as "Owner Operator" and attached it to his bathroom mirror. I designed a poster with our business name and logo, slogan, and phone number. I placed it on his closet door so he'd always see it. For myself, I had a suit custom made by a celebrity designer in preparation for my upcoming events. I even chose my hairstyle, shoes, and jewelry that I needed to complete the look. Yes, my faith is off the Richter scale and going even higher.

Examples

If you would like to get married, here are some examples of preparing to meet your significant other:

- Go pick out your wedding dress now.
- Try on the wedding dress and take pictures to review later.
- Plan every detail of your wedding.

- Make room in your closet and dresser drawers for when your partner moves in. Leave the space empty.
- Purchase books about relationships and marriages.
- During dinner, be sure to set an extra place.
- Look for relationships to admire; avoid jealousy, be truly happy for others in their relationship, and know your time for a long-lasting relationship is on the way.

This is how I implemented this technique: Before I started to date, I bought a book on marriage, written from a Christian man's point of view. At this time, I decided I needed to take care of myself; so I went to counseling to address any mental health issues that might be a hindrance in my relationships. I did that for myself, my future children, and my expected spouse. To engrain my subconscious with positive, loving relationships, I put up posters of loving couples all around my room. I left an empty space in my closet and dresser. I spoke affirmations every day.

Eventually, the love of my life and I found each other. After being in a close-knit relationship, George and I had difficulties due to his job shifting him to longer hours. This created separation anxiety and frustration between us, to the point I didn't think we were going to make it. But then, I shifted my mentality and began to pray more and think positive thoughts. I even went out and tried on a wedding dress; I took pictures of myself wearing the dress, even though we had broken up. Ultimately, we just got married at the courthouse. I just needed the love of my life in my life, and that's all that really mattered to me.

Examples
If you desire to give birth to a child, here are some actions to manifest a new bundle of joy:

- Pick out a name now.
- Start to get the nursery ready.
- Create a vision board of your desired theme.
- Get a few baby outfits. Leave them out where they can be seen.

- Purchase books about babies.
- Watch videos on baby deliveries as well as development of babies throughout the nine months.
- Decide the details of your baby shower.

This is how I implemented this technique: George, who was my boyfriend at the time, dropped a bomb on me by saying he may have difficulty fathering a child. Before, during, and after this time, I was speaking affirmations about having two to four more kids. I went as far as to write with on all of my mirrors "Two to four more kids." Every time I passed by a mirror, I would see it. Whenever I looked in the mirror, I spoke it.

Ultimately, George went to see a specialist; they told him he may need certain procedures, but then I got pregnant without it. Prior to that, we had already picked out boys and girls names, which I saved on my phone. So when we learned about our pregnancy, we already had names picked out.

Examples

If you want to travel, consider using props and get as much preparation done now for your trip. I have traveled to destinations using the following ideas:

- Get a passport if you want to travel abroad.
- Purchase a suitcase and pack it.
- Put up pictures of where you want to go as well as a list of attractions you'd like to see.

This is how I implemented this technique: For places that we wanted to visit, I posted images on my vision board and also on my phone, which I reviewed often with the help of an alarm. We got our passports without knowing the full details of our trip. We just knew we would go.

Examples

If you desire a new place or home, here are some ideas you can put into action:

- Begin to pack up your belongings now.
- Begin to look for places online or in person. Don't worry about the details.
- Begin to decorate your new place with a vision board or online decorating app. Find images online, and make a collage to see how everything goes together.
- Buy keepsake or miniature items of the thing you desire.
- Make a list of all the details you desire, such as number of bedrooms, color, location, and square footage.

This is how I implemented this technique: I used the packing method twice, without knowing where I was going or how to pay for the move. I didn't even know this was a method of the law of attraction. I just had crazy faith. I knew that God would provide. And he did, right on time. I moved from Michigan to a condo in Alabama, and then I moved from that condo to a brand-new home. Yes, I looked online for places. And yes, I did look in person. The Bible says if you seek, you shall find. Well, I found … twice, just in the nick of time. Yes, I did develop collages on my phone that became reality. I had to design my home online first and in my imagination, and it manifested.

Check Yourself

I've read many stories about people who wrote themselves a checks for a certain amount of money. Jim Carrey did this; he wrote himself a check for $10 million. Later, he manifested that amount by starring in a major movie. Another great story is where a man wrote himself a check and taped it to his ceiling. Hey, it's worth a shot, right? You have to keep an open mind, step outside the box, and get creative. You must try all options to burn your desires into your subconscious with good feelings.

Be consistent. It all depends on how serious you are about your desires. Be willing to learn, listen, and apply; most of all, stay positive, and believe that God is able to do it. He will bless you in his perfect timing. Don't just say you believe with your lips but subconsciously, you're doubting and cursing the entire process. Jesus said, don't be fooled; you will get nothing. Believe. Believe. Believe. I realize that our thought process is no match for God. It is not up to us to figure out how. We must believe and know that we know, what we know, without a shadow of doubt. God is able to do the impossible. Remember, we serve a big, big, big God.

These are just a few ideas to assist with getting creative. Again, it is important to think outside the box. You must go from believing to knowing that your request has been heard and knowing that God is orchestrating all that needs to happen to bring you your desires.

Some people may think you are crazy or weird; so what? Reverend Ike said it best when he commented that he didn't give a d**n what others had to say about him. It was pretty shocking at first to hear a pastor cursing, but I looked past that and knew he had a great point. People have gone to their graves not pursuing something because of what others would say about them. They feared what was being said behind their backs rather than focusing on their goals.

Rev. Ike goes on to say that you almost have to be delusional. That doesn't mean breaking the law or pursuing something that's not available. Delusional means believing something to be true that is clearly not. He encourages his congregation to use the stage of their imagination to really see the thing, person, or place they desire. To see it, before they see it.

Spirituality

My new motto is, "Stay ready, so you won't have to get ready." You see, if you truly believe that God will give you your heart's desire, not only will you praise him in advance, you'll prepare for your blessing by getting ready, since you truly expect it. While you are supposedly waiting on the Lord, he's waiting on you.

Be dressed in readiness, and keep your lamps lit. (Luke 12:36 NASV)

> What [does it] profit, my brethren, though a man say he hath faith, and have not works? (James 2:14 KJV)

> And all things, whatsoever ye shall ask in prayer, believing, ye shall receive. (Matthew 21:22)

Exercise

"Act as If …" is a fun tool to help manifest your desires. Below, in each of the five major life categories, note how you can start to behave, speak, think, and feel as if you already have something you want.

Example
Relationship: Don't say, "There are no good men."
Do say, "I meet great men everywhere I go."

Spiritual: _____
_____
_____
_____

Physical: _____
_____
_____
_____

Financial: _____
_____
_____
_____

Career: _____
_____
_____
_____

Relationship: _____
_____
_____
_____

10

Level Up

This chapter will discuss how to level up your mentality and advance to the next level. Leveling up is about growth and self-empowerment. It's acknowledging your failures and learning from them, moving forward with upward progress, and realizing that something greater is within you. It's about increasing your self-esteem. Some people know they have low self-esteem but do nothing about it; others are in denial about their self-worth. Whether you know it or not, your self-esteem affects every aspect of your life.

Second, your self-esteem determines what you expect to receive in life. You'll get what you expect to get out of life. Whether your expectations are conscious, subconscious, or unconscious, they can be self-fulfilling prophecies. Third, your level of self-esteem determines what you attract into your life. Remember, like attracts like is a universal law. Therefore, you must do the inner work first in to order upgrade your mentality and self-worth, then you'll be able to attract the outer results you desire.

Walk with the Wise

I cannot stress enough how important it is to mind the company you keep. According to Proverbs 13:20, he that walks with wise men shall be wise, but a companion of fools shall be destroyed. In other words, you are the company that you keep. Even if you're wise, if you have foolish friends, they will eventually destroy you. If you are foolish but have wise friends, they will show you the way to success. Although it may be difficult to let these friends go, the Bible declares that you should not be deceived; evil communication corrupts good manners.

So let this be a warning that you listen to. If you have trouble locating positive friends, no worries; I am here to help you. While the internet has a lot of evil and corruption, please know that there is a lot of good information as well. You must seek, and you will find it. There are many great leaders and successful people you can buy books from. You can listen to CDs and podcasts as well as turn your car into a mobile library. You can also follow inspiring, positive people on social media sites such as YouTube, Facebook, and Instagram. It is important that you remove the negativity from those sites and replace it with positive information. I, too, have turned my car into a mobile library, which has helped me tremendously by making good use of my commuting time.

Mobile Library

The idea of turning your car into a mobile library was inspired by one of my favorite YouTubers, Justin Perry, who developed the You Are Creators channel. He meant business when he said he was ready to change his life. He explained that he would listen to audiobooks and wrote affirmations that later manifested. He said that people would laugh at him. I can totally relate. I can only imagine how they were feeling, as they had front-row seats as he became a millionaire, a best-selling author, and a well-known YouTuber. Now he's the one laughing all the way to the bank.

People probably called him weird, but remember, you get out what you put in. I really love and respect the way he shares his knowledge and education with others. This is a great example of giving to others and helping them. All you have to do is take notes and follow instructions. I know I definitely have. I'm beginning to see great changes within myself. The mobile library idea is also a great method of increasing your mind power by making good use of time, energy, efforts, and vibrations.

Protect Yourself

Another step when you are working to level up your life is to protect your spirit. Whether you realize it or not, we are continuously being influenced by music, television, friends, and family. With all these influences and continuous interactions, it's very easy to pick up negative energies. So you have to put forth an effort to protect your spirit from contamination; limit your time with negative people. While that's vital, it's also important to increase positive influences.

As you can see, there's a number of things you can do to level up your knowledge and energy, such as books, audiobooks, and social media, but you can also find a prayer group in your local community, especially during difficult times. You can find a support group if you struggle from a trauma or tragedy. There are also prayer lines that you can call, such as 700 Club, which I've used myself. Remember, if you ask God for protection, help, and guidance, you shall receive.

Get Help

If you are having difficulties that keep you from striving and thriving in the life you desire, seek help now. Remember, pride goes before destruction. So you must be willing to set aside your pride and ask for help, whether it is mental, spiritual, physical, or emotional help. You might even want to consider a life coach. Life coaches help people to move forward and set and achieve personal and professional goals for the life they want. They are especially helpful for people who are stuck or want to make a major change in their lives.

Another great idea is to find an accountability partner. Accountability partners help you achieve your goals and assist you in your journey. They make you accept responsibility for your actions and stay true to your commitments. Sometimes, when people lack motivation, they are unaccountable; they make excuses, put things off, and never reach their goals. If you're not sure where to begin, look for leaders that resonate with you and your life; listen to their story and implement their strategies in your own life. You can also find yourself a mentor in your local community or online.

Add Value to Yourself

As you contemplate making great changes in your life, it's important to invest in yourself. Most days, we spend our money frivolously on things that add no value to our lives, such as phones, clothes, shoes, purses, and cars. These things will all lose their value. Yes, I do it too. While all those things have their place, they should never come before investing in yourself. An investment in yourself never loses value; it only increases your self-worth and self-esteem. The following suggestions are just a few ways you can invest in yourself:

- Attend self-development seminars and conferences.
- Hire a life coach.
- Read self-development books.
- Enroll in a vocational training or certificate program.

Always remember, education is everything, because knowledge is power. While pursing my undergraduate degree, I considered pursuing a doctoral degree. However, after receiving my MBA, I thought I was done with education forever. After earning my last degree, I felt exhausted. In retrospect, I should have attended seminars, workshops, and conferences. We should keep learning all of our lives, no matter how young or old, in an effort to stay green in our minds (meaning fresh and up to date). The fact of the matter is, we should always be improving. This will allow us to stay inspired, encouraged, and motivated.

You may say you want a change in your life, but you have to make a change within yourself first. You have to take action. You have to put your money where your mouth is. You must take a leap of faith and trust in God. You must take the risk because you are worth the risk. Yes, you are destined for greatness. For a long time, I struggled with feeling like I was not enough. But now, I know that I am more than enough because I am a child of God. God loves me, and he loves you too. I now know that I am worthy of the greatness that God has in store for me. Remember, you are too. Keep telling yourself that until you actually begin to believe it, feel it, and know it. Remember, you have the power and authority to speak life over yourself. Use your words wisely because you can either add or subtract value to yourself; you decide which, today and every day.

My Level-Up Experience

If I knew then what I know now, I would have found a way to invest in myself because the results are mind-blowing, but to this day, I still look at my life and see how it has unfolded to everything that I have spoken, written, affirmed, and focused on the most. We live and learn from our own shortcomings, and we make improvements from that point on, while helping others down the correct path.

I returned to the same law of attraction coaching academy, but my initial coach was no longer there. They assigned me someone else, and it was immediately apparent that she was new. In my mind, she was too new for me, especially since I considered myself experienced, so I sought out the founder of the academy; however, she no offered private coaching at the time. She was doing groups, books, and podcasts. I decided to purchase one of her package deals, which included a couple of books, a workbook, and meditation recordings. You see, I decided I was worth investing into. You must know and believe that you are worth the investment, worth the change, worth the elevation, worth the new knowledge, and worth the education. You have to come to that realization. If you keep doing the same thing, you will keep getting the same results. Expecting anything else is the definition of insanity. You must focus, and you must get serious. Remember, the choice is yours. You decide the outcome of your life.

If you have a habit that is consuming too much of your time but not adding value to your life, replace it with a good one; start by using the alarm on your phone to schedule time for spiritual development. This will ensure that you remove negative habits and replace them with positive ones. Perhaps your bad habit is watching too much TV, spending too much time on social media, gossiping on the phone, or something else. You can simply replace that bad habit with a good one, such as reading self-help books, watching positive videos, listening to wholesome audiobooks, praying, meditating, speaking affirmations, and so much more. Studies have shown that it can take from twenty-one to forty-five days to form a new habit. If you put positive actions into practice, they will eventually become habits. You will begin to see results, and so will others. It can drastically change your life. It can help elevate your vibration and find your true higher self.

My Musical Inspiration

The name of this chapter, "Level Up," was inspired by Ciara, one of my favorite R&B artists. I love everything about her: her beauty, her voice, her music, her style, and her dance moves; I mean everything. I recently fell even more in love with her; her song, "Level Up," discusses how she handled the ending of a relationship. Some of the lyrics to "Level Up" (2018) are listed below. The complete set of lyrics can be found at: www. azlyrics.com/lyrics/ciara/levelup.html:

> Them old mistakes are gone
> I won't do them no more
> That's old news, there's new news.
>
> I turned nothing to something,
> my comeback on one hunnit.
>
> I just keep elevating
> No losses, just upgrading
> My lessons, made blessings.

This inspirational song shows how she made mistakes but learned from them. God delivered her from less into a better place of blessings. It exhibits her growth and maturity. It speaks of her higher mindset. It proves how she spoke (and still speaks) life and how she came back stronger to win on a higher level. Unfortunately, negative people misconstrued the message and assumed she was speaking about previous relationship. In my opinion, she wasn't talking about anyone specific; rather, she came to the conclusion that she deserved better, so she got better, along with more blessings. She eventually explained how she was inspired by a pastor's message; she was simply saying we should love ourselves, and by doing so, she was upgraded and being treated the way she deserved to be treated.

I can attest to the importance of loving yourself; it upgraded me to the life I live today, with a beautiful, loving relationship with my life partner, life companion, best friend, and husband, George. I took some time to love on myself, which included getting healthy, losing weight, seeking mental health assistance, and getting closer spiritually to God. After I began loving myself, my heart, mind, body, and spirit, God blessed me really good. He blessed me with one of his own angels on earth, who treats me like a queen.

So again, I can really attest to what Ciara is saying, and that it is really true. Many times, we want to get something right now and just settle for less, even though God knows we are worth so much more; if we don't know it ourselves, it doesn't matter. You get what you expect. You must take your thinking and your thoughts to a higher level. Remember, if you keep doing the same thing, you will continue to get the same results. So level up today.

Spirituality

The Word of God even tells us to renew our mind, which will result in our transformation:

> And be not conformed to this world: but be ye transformed by the renewing of your mind, that ye may prove what is that good, and acceptable, and perfect, will of God. (Romans 12:2 KJV)

> And be renewed in the spirit of your mind. (Ephesians 4:23 KJV)

Exercise

After reading this chapter, what methods do you intend to implement within your own life in order to level up?

Spiritual: _____

_____

_____

_____

_____

Physical: _____

_____

_____

_____

_____

Financial: _____

_____

_____

_____

_____

Career: _____

_____

_____

_____

_____

Relationship: _____

_____

_____

_____

_____

_____

11

Release Negativity

Throughout this book, I explain the importance of dispersing positive vibrations in every aspect of your life, but I'd like to address a crucial topic when it comes to manifesting. You must clear out all the deep-seated issues that cause negativity in your life. This negativity is called resistance. Resistance usually take the form of subconscious fears, doubts, or any other negative emotion, all of which can create a blockage of energy that hinders manifesting your desires.

It also creates a vicious cycle of negativity that can be challenging to get rid of. When trying to manifest your desires by using any of the law of attraction methods, you may get some results but not quite what you desired; that's because you are weighed down by resistance. Resistance could come in the following forms:

- pride
- anger
- fear
- grief
- apathy
- guilt
- shame
- sadness
- powerlessness
- any other negative emotion

By fully releasing resistance, applying forgiveness, or using another healing method, you stop fueling limited beliefs and begin to funnel that powerful energy towards something more productive. For example, if a pipe is clogged, you wouldn't continue to pour more liquid down it; instead, you would first remove the clog and allow the flow to work properly at its full capacity. This is the same process that must take place within your spirit. If you fail to remove the blockage within your spirit, you will not operate at your full potential; in fact, negative emotions could cause dysfunctions mentally, spiritually, relationally, financially, and even physically, to you as well as the people connected to you. All because you refuse, ignore, deny, deflect, or avoid the needed repair(s) within yourself. There's an exercise at the end of this chapter to help you start releasing resistance.

No matter the circumstances, you must make all efforts to release these low-vibrational energies. It's important that you forgive yourself as well as others. Forgiveness is love in action. Remember that manifestation depends on the emotional state you are currently in. You are always attracting and manifesting, whether positive or negative; intentionally or not. If you are in a negative emotional state, you are manifesting things you don't want. If you are in positive emotions, that means you are manifesting things you do want. You have the power to choose and change by shifting your emotions. While I don't claim to be an expert at releasing resistance, I know it's extremely important for your spirituality. I know that the Bible warns against negative emotions because they can defile your spirit (Mark 7:21–23). God desires purity in our flesh as well as in our spirit. The Word of God promotes the seven fruits of the Spirit of God, as follows (Galatians 5:22–23):

- love
- joy
- peace
- patience
- kindness
- goodness
- faithfulness
- gentleness
- self-control

Let It Burn

I do know what has worked for me: much prayer, praise, and worship as well as reading, studying, and being a doer of the Word of God. I have even written lengthy letters to express negative emotions towards a person and then promptly burned the letter, with the intention of releasing the negative emotions. To my surprise, it worked, and I felt a sense of relief. I didn't know until later that this was a law of attraction technique. Even if I don't have strong negative emotions, I still do the exercise for anyone who conjures any type of bad feeling. I have become serious about manifesting my desires. This method is harmless, safe, easy, yet powerful for any emotional healing you need.

You simply write a letter to the person, whether alive or deceased, you have negative feelings towards. It could be an ex-lover, parent, spouse, work colleague, or anyone. You are writing as if you were speaking to their face; tell them what they did and how it made you feel. Don't hold back because no one will read this except you. Take as much time as needed, even if it takes a few days to remember everything. This is a safe and harmless way to express your emotions, so don't feel any regret or guilt.

After you've written the letter, read it out loud, with feeling, and then burn it in a safe place, such as a fireplace or large ceramic bowl or in the sink. As the letter begins to burn, say aloud, "I release, burn, and clear all negativity within this letter, in the name of your creator." Just bask in the healing and relief of the pain, and receive it in your spirit. I would advise you do this as much as needed, until you feel an inner peace. So let it burn and allow all negative emotions to disintegrate.

Let Go, Let God

I have tried other methods of clearing resistance, such as meditation and affirmations. I've even gone to counseling to help work through my issues. Talk with an expert in mental health or a spiritual leader, such as a pastor you trust. It's important not to ignore, suppress, distract, or avoid those negative emotions; release them completely. When you ignore or suppress negative emotions, it allows negative energy to accumulate, which can later manifest into physical ailments.

If you express negative emotions, it could result in anger, violence, or fighting, only to provide little relief; it will make the situation worse. Some people avoid negative emotions by replacing them with a quick fix such as painkillers, alcohol, sex, or another self-destructive activity;

this is the most common way to escape painful inner negativity. It only makes matters worse. So let go, and let God take control.

Step in Their Shoes

During my examination of releasing resistance, I discovered another technique, as written by Gleb Esman (2018), to release negative emotions for the purpose of correctly manifesting your desires. Rather than releasing negative emotions, you can transcend negativity by dismantling the foundation of negative emotions. It may provide more emotional relief than releasing emotions. The process of releasing emotions may or may not work; however, if you transcend emotions, they are said to go away for good. Before this powerful process can work, you must discover what caused the emotion.

Situation/Event/Condition --> Our Interpretation --> Emotion.

When a situation happens, your mind interprets the occurrence and applies a subjective interpretation of the situation. By consciously changing your interpretation of a situation, you transcend emotions, meaning transcending resistance, thus allowing proper manifestation. I definitely recommend this technique. You simply take a walk in their shoes, meaning look at the situation from their point of view: challenges, thought processes, and experiences could increase your compassion and help you understand why things happened in the first place. Not only will it elevate your understanding and compassion, it will also help you to empathize with their perspective or point of view before being quick to judge people for their actions. This technique is a biblical application of bearing the burden of your brothers and sisters in Christ by showing empathy.

Use real-life examples.

	Situation	My Interpretation	Emotion
#1	I was raised in a single-mother home; Dad was in prison for twenty-eight years.	I did not have a stable male role model in my home while growing up.	Neglected

Transcending

My father, in fact, considered my needs and well-being, so he took major risks to provide for his family.

By consciously changing my interpretation of the situation, I remove the negative emotion of neglect; therefore, removing resistance.

Spirituality

Below I have compiled a few biblical scriptures relating to the effects of negative emotions on one's heart, soul, and body.

A glad heart makes a cheerful face, but by sorrow of
heart the spirit is crushed. (Proverbs 15:13 ESV)

A tranquil heart gives life to the flesh, but envy
makes the bones rot. (Proverbs 14:30 ESV)

A joyful heart is good medicine, but a crushed spirit
dries up the bones. (Proverbs 17:22 ESV)

Anxiety in a man's heart weighs him down, but a good
word makes him glad. (Proverbs 12:25 ESV)

Exercise

Are there any negative emotions in the following areas of your life that need to be released or transcended? If yes, using the information and example above, provide details on how you can release or transcend those negative emotions.

Spiritual: _____

_____

_____

_____

_____

Physical: _____

_____

_____

_____

_____

Financial: _____

_____

_____

_____

_____

Career: _____

_____

_____

_____

_____

Relationship: _____

_____

_____

_____

12

Love in Action: Giving

G iving and receiving are equally important. It is a natural exchange of energies in the universe or a spiritual exchange of power of God. God (or the universe) loves when we take part of the flow of giving and taking. According to the law of attraction, giving indicates there is abundance in the universe; therefore, plenty to go around. By not giving, you are proving to the universe there is scarcity; there is not enough to go around. Giving is a key principle in the law of attraction, but it's sometimes left out, and people don't manifest their desires as they'd like to. Giving is the key that unlocks the door of blessings. If you have a clear desire that you'd like to manifest, you must believe that it is in the spiritual realm, and when it appears in the physical, it becomes evident for everyone to see. It means you received your blessing, request, wish, desire from God.

What to Give?

So what do you have to give? There are many ways to give back to others in need. Money is always great to give, but you can give in other ways too. You can give away clothing, shoes, furniture, food, and so much more. It does not stop there; you can give your time by volunteering with others who are less fortunate than you. Make sure you give from the heart, not grudgingly. Remember, God knows your heart and your motive when no one else does. According to 2 Corinthians 9:7 (KJV), "God loveth a cheerful giver."

Open Your Hand, Open Your Heart

Does that mean that you give everything you have? No. You give according to your budget, your spirit, your need, or what is in your heart. For instance, if you have five dollars, you can give a stranger a dollar. I know people who would look at this simple scenario and speak into the atmosphere that they are broke and do not have much to give. They would hold on to it tightly and not share at all. There are some people who are so tight with money that they squeak when they walk, but those same people are looking for handouts and freebies. Remember, a closed hand can't receive, and a closed heart can't give.

Tithing

If you are a Christian, are you expected to follow the Word of God and pay tithes and offerings? Tithing is donating a tenth, or 10 percent, of your income to your religious organization. The Bible goes on to say that many people rob God himself because of their failure to pay their tithes and offerings. It says you will be cursed; that sounds extremely scary to me.

So why don't some people pay tithes and offerings? Some say they cannot afford it. One of my spiritual leaders always said, "You cannot afford not to pay," meaning that the effect of the curse would bring about scarcity, cause barrenness, and make holes in your pockets. Thank God, I cannot tell you the effect of the curse, because I am a proud and faithful tither; therefore, I have only experienced the blessings and living in the overflow. I am honestly afraid not to pay, because I've seen marvelous things take place in my life since I began tithing consistently.

Many people miss out on the point and opportunity to tithe.

- Tithing is about obedience.
- Tithing is about love.
- Tithing is about faith.

They tend to focus on the wrong things. They're concerned about how the finances of the church are being managed. They think the church leaders are mismanaging funds, and this negates their obligation to God regarding giving tithes and offerings; however, they are wrong. We all have to be accountable for own doings, whether right or wrong. You do your part, and God will handle the rest. My advice is to find a church you believe in and plant your tithes, offerings, and seeds.

Harvest Time

That leads me to my next point on seed offering. A seed offering is another way to give. A seed offering is a form of giving for the future existence of one's desire, by saying thank you in advance for what you're about to receive. Everything in life starts with a seed. A seed faith offering reflects the process of reaping and sowing. It is giving an amount above the tithe and offering. It is the seed of faith that we plant as evidence of our faith to God. Luke 6:38 says, "Give, and it will be given to you." You must first plant a seed of faith, and God will multiply it back to you to meet your needs and desires. So you must believe the Lord hears your prayers and expect him to bless you according to your faith. If you plant a little, you'll reap a little; the opposite is also true.

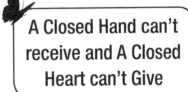

A Closed Hand can't receive and A Closed Heart can't Give

So what if you don't have faith, but you desire to manifest something? Well, it won't work. God says you must believe when you pray or make your request. The principles of the law of attraction require belief, too. The law of attraction goes hand in hand. Yes, God blesses the just as well as the unjust, but how much more will he give to you when you are obedient in your giving and believe in the process and in him? You can increase your faith by reading the Word of God. It is written in the Bible, "So then faith cometh by hearing and hearing by the word of God" (Romans 10:17 KJV). You must also take heed to the Word by being a doer; if you test God to prove his Word is true, he will open the floodgates of heaven and pour out an overflow of blessing upon you.

My Experience in Giving

Let me start by saying that this part of the law of attraction and Word of God was easier than it may have been for others, because it is a part my personality. I am a natural giver. My primary motivation is to take care of others, to make sure they are well. To me, it feels good to help out and give; God always restores me. Since I grew up in a Baptist church, I witnessed the act of placing money in the basket; however, I never learned what it meant until I joined Holy Trinity Church of God in Christ, a Pentecostal church in Muskegon, MI, where Bishop Nathanial Wells explained about tithing in great detail, including its miraculous effect. I still remember how he challenged the non-tithers, which at the time included me, to consistently pay tithes and offerings for at least three years and to watch how God would open up the windows of heaven and pour out his blessing.

I took the challenge, trusting the Word of God and my pastor's teaching. It worked, and it didn't take three years; within six months, my life began to transform. I have been blessed ever since, and I pay consistently no matter what. I did not allow trials or tribulations to hinder my dedication to God's Word regarding tithes, but that doesn't mean I wasn't tempted. I made many mistakes in life, but I knew I could be perfect in at least one area: I could be a perfect tither. So I am reaping all the blessings and expecting many more on the way.

During my initial learning process of tithing and the blessings God has to offer, I also learned about seed faith offerings. That is the ultimate expression of faith to God, to put your money where your mouth is. Many people say they believe, but do they really? Some people say this is just a way to line the pastor's pockets. That's the furthest from the truth. They encourage tithes and offerings because they have seen wonderful testimonies. Just make sure you are planting your seed in good, holy ground.

Spirituality

The word *give* appears 921 times in the Bible. That is almost as much as "faith" (270), "hope" (165), and "love" (541) added together. Giving is love in action. Giving is an expression of faith, hope, and love. So what does all this mean? It means giving is very important. Below, I have listed various religious scriptures that pertain to the importance of giving. The common thread among Christianity, Islam, Buddhism, and Hinduism is in alignment with the law of attraction:

It also says "He which soweth sparingly, shall reap also sparingly; and he which soweth bountifully shall reap also bountifully." It goes on to say "Give generously to them and do so without a grudging heart; then because of this the LORD your God will bless you in all your work and in everything you put your hand to." (2 Corinthians 9:6)

Give, even if you only have a little. (Buddha)

Those who spend in Charity will be richly rewarded. (Quran 57:10)

Those who (in charity) spend of their goods by night and by day, in secret and in public, have their reward with their Lord: on them shall be no fear, nor shall they grieve. (Quran 2:274)

The Law of Giving is very simple:
If you want joy, give joy.
If love is what you seek, offer love.
If you crave material affluence, help others
become prosperous. (Deepak Chopra)

I hope you understood my explanation and will immediately start to implement the practice of giving, as it is a commandment from our Lord God as well as in alignment with the laws of the universe. To help you start the process, I have added an exercise for you to complete.

GIVE!

GIVE!

GIVE!

Exercise

In this chapter, you have gained valuable knowledge about giving and how it can greatly determine how you manifest. What have you given this week in the following major areas of life? If nothing, ask yourself what you can give next week. What do you desire? Is it love or money? Be sure to give just that.

Spiritual: _____
_____
_____
_____

Physical: _____
_____
_____
_____
_____

Financial: _____
_____
_____
_____
_____

Career: _____
_____
_____
_____
_____

Relationship: _____
_____
_____
_____

CONCLUSION

Throughout this book, I have explained how I applied the Word of God and used the law of attraction to manifest my heart's desires of people, places, events, and career, after being bound with resistance. I followed by intuition, sought God for help, and put in the work in order to break free from negativity. Like many, I am still a work in progress; however, I am declaring complete healing in my heart, mind, soul, and every aspect of my life as well as those connected to me. The Bible said I received not because I asked not (James 4:3) and that if I asked, I would receive (Matthew 7:7). I simply asked God, my Father in heaven, and believed; I expected my blessing according to his will and his way.

You see, God had already given me the power and authority; I just needed to operate in it. On a daily basis, I spoke life by using decrees and declarations, calling forth my desires from the spiritual realm into the physical world. Please take note that I did not beg or plead to God; however, I made my requests known to him (Philippians 4:6). Remember, I believed, I knew, and I began to thank him in advance for bringing my requests to pass, in his perfect timing (Mark 11:24). Here is my motto:

> "I claim it, I believe it, I see it, and I receive it. In Jesus's name, Amen."

Because of my faith, the next important step was to take action (James 2:17), which meant that I needed to do everything humanly possible, and God would do the rest. In my case, it was self-care, which meant mental health counseling, doctor visits, reading my Bible, joining the choir, exercising, journaling, and finding an accountability partner. I encouraged myself in the Lord often, no matter what the situation looked like. I had been through a lot in my life and knew that God did not bring me this far to leave me. By implementing the knowledge I revealed, you can transform your life by acknowledging your power within. No one said it would be easy; however, it is possible, with perseverance, and it will be worthwhile.

Each of these chapters offers some powerful principles with effective methods and strategies that you can use to realize your greatness within. Move forward in your life with your new awareness and utilize your power and authority to break free from any traps holding you back. The better your awareness, the better choices in life, which leads to better results. First, take a moment to contemplate your life now and imagine where you'd like it to be. Unlock the power of your vivid imagination to see your future. Then you decide what you'd like the end result to be. Remember, vague requests lead to vague answers, so be sure to get down to the nitty-gritty of your desires.

Begin to speak positively about your wishes to yourself and anyone who will listen. Make sure to keep your thoughts aligned with your aspirations. You can even have some fun manifesting by taking a pen and paper, and writing your very own script about your dreams, starring you, of course. While going through the scripting process, a smile should come across your face, invoking positive feelings. Simply take a moment to say, "Thank you," in advance for what you expect to come and what you already have. Depending on your faith level, prepare for your manifestation as much as possible. Before you know it, things will begin to unfold, revealing what you've been yearning for.

Now you've heard of the transformation in my life, from my isolated cocoon of pain to becoming a beautiful butterfly, soaring in my purpose. It didn't happen until I learned how to apply the Word of God to my everyday life. We should also know that we serve a God who is the same yesterday, today, and forever more; however, our society has drastically changed. So how do we get the most out of the Word of God, which contains powerful instructions and promises, and which clearly states that we have power and authority? God has given us power and authority in the following areas, just to name a few:

- the power of thoughts
- the power to speak life
- the power of imagination
- the power to write the vision
- the power of sound mind
- the power of choice (free will)
- the power of emotions

Many people don't know how to utilize their God-given energy or even operate within the laws of the universe. No matter your beliefs, religion, or race, we are all human beings. We are made up of energy, just like everything around us. We are all connected to a higher power, greater than anything we could ever imagine. Whether we believe in these laws or not, they are at work at all times. We can continue to operate on default and think that things are happening to us, when, in fact, we ourselves are attracting situations and circumstances, consciously and subconsciously. Or we can become aware of our powerful abilities and use them to our advantage.

We need a way in which we can effectively apply biblical knowledge on a daily basis. Yes, of course, there is much power in fervent prayer. But how about the rest of the day, when you're not on your knees in prayer, talking to God? This is where the law of attraction's techniques can greatly assist Christians and others looking to manifest their heart's desires. Techniques are simply practical skills for everyone to use. The law of attraction can be used for anyone with any belief; it's a universal law, and since we are all part of this universe, it also applies to you. You can just customize the techniques to meet your beliefs. For instance, if you are a Christian, you are speaking declarations to God going through Jesus Christ.

As a result of reading this book, you can turn your life around by applying your beliefs using the law of attraction's techniques. By consistently applying these techniques and using your own beliefs, you'll be able to manifest your heart's desires in no time. The key is that you must believe, and you must be consistent and in total alignment with your subconscious, your conscious mind, your words, your thoughts, your emotions, and your actions. You will begin to reveal the hidden treasures within yourself like never before. Take full advantage of the exercises after each chapter to help you start activating your power today.

If you do not have a savior, I hope my experience resonates with you to make the choice to give Jesus Christ, my Lord and Savior, a try. For he is Sovereign, Kings of kings, Lord of lords, Alpha and Omega, Prince of Peace, Creator, Light of the World, redeemer, and the Holy One. He died on the cross for you and me. He is the way and the truth and the life (John 14:6). God gave his only begotten Son, Jesus, so that whoever believes in him would not perish but have eternal life (John 3:16). You cannot get to God, the Father, except you go through the Son, Jesus (1 John 2:23). Many try to avoid, deny, and ignore Jesus Christ, who I believe to be the one and only true God, but there will come a time when every knee shall bend and every tongue shall confess that Jesus Christ is Lord, to the glory of God the Father (Philippians 2:11).

I am a first-hand witness that Jesus is alive, well, and powerful. Many people seek a higher power to fill their empty void and ease their pain. I encourage you to seek after Jesus Christ, for he is the only one who can quench your thirst. Be not deceived; whoever is not with Jesus is against him (Matthew 12:30). While I respect your right to serve who you please, I hope you will choose correctly; as for me and my household, we shall serve the Lord (Joshua 24:15).

Each of us is given a measure of grace, but don't abuse the grace of God, thinking you have all the time in the world because you do not. Choose this day who you will serve because tomorrow is not promised to any of us; no one knows when their appointed time will come around, nor do we know when Judgment Day is upon us. Do not wait until it's too late. Repent your sins and be saved by Jesus Christ now. Seek the Lord while he may still be found.

Reminders:

- ☐ Stay positive.
- ☐ Get crystal clear on your desires.
- ☐ Always have your vision before you; create a vision board.
- ☐ Be sure to forgive, and only remember the lesson.
- ☐ Always invest in yourself; you're worth it.
- ☐ Instead of getting ready, stay ready.
- ☐ Give, give, give.
- ☐ Always speak life.
- ☐ Have the audacity to think and dream big.
- ☐ Believe that all things are possible with God.
- ☐ Use music to increase spirit's vibration.
- ☐ Find a mentor, accountability partner, or life coach.
- ☐ Become disciplined.
- ☐ Ask for help, as needed.

BIBLIOGRAPHY

Abraham-Hicks, by Jerry and Esther Hicks. "Ask and It Is Given: Learning to Manifest Your Desires." The Emotional Guidance System. AbrahamHicks.com, 2004.

Byrne, Rhonda. *The Secret*. New York, Hillsboro, Oregon: Atria Books, Beyond Words Publishing, 2006.

Esman, Gleb. *Law of Attraction: How to Deal with Negative Emotions*. 2018.

Morin, Amy. "7 Scientifically Proven Benefits of Gratitude That Will Motivate You To Give Thanks Year-Round." *Forbes*, Nov. 23, 2014. https://www.forbes.com/sites/amymorin/2014/11/23/7-scientifically-proven-benefits-of-gratitude-that-will-motivate-you-to-give-thanks-year-round/#2057ee4183c0

Orloff, Judith. *Emotional Freedom: Liberate Yourself From Negative Emotions and Transform Your Life*. Three Rivers Press, 2011. https://www.psychologytoday.com/us/blog/emotional-freedom/201102/what-is-your-emotional-type